WWW.PASSAICPUBLICLIBRARY.ORG
D1082751

THE BOOK

Burkhard Spinnen

THE BOOK

AN HOMAGE

Illustrations by Line Hoven

Translated by Aaron Kerner

David R. Godine · *Publisher*

BOSTON

Published in 2018 by
DAVID R. GODINE · *Publisher*
Post Office Box 450
Jaffrey, New Hampshire 03452
www.godine.com

First Published as Das Buch by Schöffling & Co.
in Frankfurt am Main in 2016

The translation of this work was supported by
a grant from the Goethe-Institut.

LIBRARY OF CONGRESS CATALOGING-IN-PUBLICATION DATA
Names: Spinnen, Burkhard, 1956– author. | Hoven, Line, illustrator.
Title: The book : an homage / Burkhard Spinnen ;
with illustrations by Line Hoven ;
translated from the German by Aaron Kerner.
Other titles: Buch. English.
Description: Jaffrey, New Hampshire : David R. Godine, 2017.
Identifiers: LCCN 2017039168 | ISBN 9781567926071 (alk. paper)
Subjects: LCSH: Books and reading. | Books—Psychological aspects. |
Libraries.
Classification: LCC Z1003 .S758613 2017 | DDC 028/.9—dc23
LC record available at https://lccn.loc.gov/2017039168

FIRST EDITION
Printed in the United States

I dedicate this book to my publishers,
Ida and Klaus Schöffling.
Twenty-five years ago
they gathered me into their world of books,
always treated and cared for me well—
they read me thoroughly,
found most of it good,
and carefully corrected the remainder.
I am eternally grateful
to them both.

TABLE OF CONTENTS

ON THE TRADE

THE BOOK COLLECTION

FOREWORD TO THE AMERICAN EDITION

EVERY AUTHOR longs to have his book translated into other languages. And I'm no exception; yet I have to say, I was especially keen to see my book on the Book published abroad. Indeed, I was almost certain that it *would* happen, since all over the world, wherever books are written, printed, and read, people today are discussing the possibility that in the immediate future the printed book will find itself displaced by the E-book. Just as the book is a global phenomenon, so is digitalization and its consequences. Presumably this evolution will proceed in various fashions in various places; but when all's said and done, it comes down to a single question: which will be the last format left standing, the paper book with printed characters, or the digital reading device for electronic files?

Thus, when the news came that my book would be translated for an American readership (and thereby for the many millions who speak English), I was absolutely delighted! For now I was able to enjoy the notion that I'd be able to share my thoughts on the book with many more people, and that they would be able to enrich and enlarge those thoughts with their own.

In the run-up to the translation, I was told that it might be important to alter certain details, so as to make the text more comprehensible to readers and bibliophiles outside of Germany. I immediately concurred. In the end, to take one example, it isn't so very important exactly which book is *my* favorite or *my* most expensive; much more important to remember that many readers maintain a special relationship to the books that are especially dear to *them*, or for which *they've* had to pay through the nose. Whether that favorite book is German or American is beside the point.

But once I finally had the American translation in my hands, it turned out that such alterations to the text weren't really necessary. My favorite book was, in fact, a French photo-book, which I'd originally read in a German translation—and of which there exists an English edition as well. Among the books I received for my First Communion and which formed my first little library, were the internationally-renowned adventure novels of Karl May, Fenimore Cooper's *Leatherstocking Tales*, and the stories of the Greek gods and heroes, the common inheritance of all humanity, as well as the cartoons of Wilhelm Busch, long known throughout the world as a forerunner of modern-day comics. And as for the first books I bought for myself with my allowance, not a few of them were novels by American authors of the Beat Generation.

What I'm trying to say is that the biography of any reader in the second half of the twentieth century is likely to be a global biography. This applies not only to the texts, but also for the ways in which one acquires books and, once they've been acquired, how one deals with them; how one collects them, loans them, or gives them as gifts. In a certain sense, we've all grown up together as readers and bibliophiles, brothers and sisters, no matter where in the world we were born. It may be that, in Europe, new books are individually wrapped in transparent plastic, and in America, not. Such things are trifles that don't really count when compared with the great, world-spanning culture of Books.

My very warm thanks to David R. Godine, Publisher, and the translator, Aaron Kerner, for opening the road for my memories and reflections on the book to the great Anglo-Saxon readership. And I wish this book, as I do books in general, all the best for the future.

Burkhard Spinnen
Münster, August 2017

ON THE WHOLE

HORSES AND BOOKS

Toward the end of the 19th century, the great cities of the world were as full of coaches and horse-carts as today they are of automobiles. Anyone who lived on a major thoroughfare, and could afford it, would spread straw on the streets to dampen the racket of iron-bound cart-wheels and horse-hooves on cobblestones. There were some 80,000 horses living in Manhattan in the year 1880; in London at the turn of the last century there were around 300,000; in Berlin during the same period there were 30,000 horses drawing omnibuses and cabs; the *Berlin Post* alone maintained around 1,600 horses.

In the cities, horses were ubiquitous. When evening came, some would return to the still rustic suburbs, but many others spent their nights in town. Depending on their owners and use, they were lodged in self-contained stables, or in annexes built over the rear courtyards of the huge apartment buildings. The *Post*, and various transport businesses like the Berlin Milk Delivery Service of the Bolle Company, owned multi-story stables in the middle of the city, the animals led to the upper floors along staircases with broad, flat risers.

Each day, along with food for the city's population, enormous quantities of fodder arrived. In 1900, the horses of London devoured around 1,200 tons of oats and 2,000 tons of hay daily. In order to deal with the resulting dung—around fifteen kilos per horse per day—a whole recycling system had to be developed; the manure was collected and used as fertilizer, but also dried out and repurposed as fuel. Nevertheless, by the 1880s there was already a fear that before long the city would be smothered in horse-dung. And horses were dying in the cities, dozens each day. Whereupon their fellow creatures dragged them to the knacker's yard. In special butcher's shops they were processed into food; thus, in another sense, horses entered the city.

From 1900 until the first world war, by contrast, automobiles were a rarity and a curiosity in the cities. In the countryside one saw almost no motor-driven vehicles whatsoever. Had anyone in those years predicted that at some point in the foreseeable future the car and the tractor would entirely supplant the horse, he would surely have generated a good deal of controversy, and perhaps even scorn. Presumably one could agree that motorization might have certain advantages here or there, but you'd have to be a fool to believe that mankind would ever be able to do without the horse. If I close my eyes and hark back to the years around 1900, I can hear all the arguments: the automobile is too expensive, too dangerous, and too complicated; it's terribly loud, and emits a revolting stench. Besides (and this was perhaps the strongest argument), in contrast to the horse, the automobile is an apparatus entirely lacking a nimbus, an aura.

And I certainly understand this resistance to mechanization. It emerged entirely naturally from the depths of the culture's experience. People around 1900 simply couldn't imagine life without horses. For centuries—no, millennia—cultures the world over had grown to greatness with the horse as their most important animal auxiliary. Only by means of horses could men and goods be conveyed across great tracts of country. They were essential aids in heavy labor. No cathedrals, no castles, no bridges could have been built without them. And finally, without horses agriculture could hardly have kept humankind fed.

Hence the possession of horses had been, since time immemorial, one of the major symbols of prosperity, strength, and importance. Kings had themselves painted on horseback. Up to the present day, horses adorn the coats of arms of aristocrats and kingdoms. Even democratic entities, like the German federal states of Lower Saxony and Northrhine-Westfalia, feature horses on their official seals. A man with a horse was not merely a stronger, but also a better, a more noble man. A knight was a horseman—that is to say, a *chevalier*.

Finally, when it came to warfare, the horse had always been the best guarantee of strength and superiority. Even during the American Civil War, it wasn't artillery, but rather a well-organized cavalry charge that was seen as the ultimate weapon. And even if, in those days, the advantage of infantry rifles over charging horses was already beginning to be demonstrated, the military leadership held fast to the old doctrine of the superiority of the cavalry until the First World War. Even today, this conviction lingers in a metaphor: anyone demanding the use of overwhelming force will talk about *calling in the cavalry.*

Yet now we smile at the loyalty and faith that people had for their horses. Because their beliefs have been proven completely wrong. In fact, the 19th century was the final century of the horse. In his book *Farewell to the Horse*, Ulrich Raulff has so gorgeously and movingly described that century that he may just awaken a yearning for it in the reader. Still, after 1900 the horse disappeared—in the blink of an eye, we might say, from an historical perspective. They vanished from the cities, the countryside, and the armies, while at the same time cars, trucks, tractors, and tanks took over their duties. By 1938, there were already over three million registered motor-vehicles in Germany; by now, there are over sixty million. The last remaining cavalry unit in the Red Army—preserved as an historical curiosity—was finally disbanded in the 1950s. For anyone visiting Vienna today, the few fiacres at their stands seem like whimsical museum exhibits. If a coach were to drive past your front door, hoofs clapping the pavement, everyone would rush to the windows in astonishment, shaking their heads.

Whenever anybody sees a horse still serving men the way it served them for thousands of years, they spontaneously think: how quaint! And immediately afterwards: how was that even possible? How could we have based the smooth functioning and preservation of society on the comparatively humble backs of such skittish and delicate creatures?

Horses, those lovely, long-suffering animals, without which we could never have built our civilization, have today found their final preserve in the Western

World as living hobbies. They are well-groomed and well-treated, often even beloved, especially by girls and young women—that is, by those who had been the most thoroughly barred from the old world of horses, almost exclusively a world of men. It's as if we were trying to atone, through a few specimens of the species, for what we have done to many millions of their fellows whom we harnessed, wore out, mistreated, whipped, and in innumerable mounted wars literally ground down, starved, and tore to pieces. But in any case: in this part of the world, the horse is history.

And now, some hundred years after mechanical conveyances demonstrated their ability to "conquer" the horse in everyday life, just as in war, we find ourselves asking anew whether an equally modern contrivance will supersede and replace an old companion of mankind. What's at issue here is the e-book. Will text break free of its paper vehicle? Will future reading take place on digital devices—monitors, tablets, or smart-phones?

Often in these debates over the future I hear voices declaring "No!" with utter conviction. Sure, they continue, the e-book has this or that advantage, but will never be able to replace the printed book. The book is such an important, indeed perhaps even the essential, expression of our culture and civilization. The book has tradition and aura; it embodies distinction and value. And therefore, they say, we will never relinquish it. If only because we *can't*.

I'd like to believe it. But then it occurs to me how quickly and easily we abandoned the horse. The mechanization and mobilization of our lives in the 19th and

20th centuries were inexorable; today it is computerization and digitalization, whose relatively late spawn is the e-book. In many areas of our everyday communications, reading texts on stationary or mobile screens, without printed paper, is already the norm. Who still writes letters, when e-mails, just barely drafted, are already with their recipients, who read them instantly on their screens? Interoffice communications, the exchange of scientific data—all this is barely imaginable anymore without digital transmission.

As one would expect, the literary world has mounted the strongest resistance against digitalization; one might say that its representatives are the last knights of the print world. Yet there are significant reasons to think that here, too, the Gutenberg Era is drawing to a close. In the end, the car and the tractor, not to mention the tank, didn't replace the horse by chance, but rather because of their strength, their stamina, and a certain undemandingness. There are also good arguments for the e-book.

Nevertheless, I would prefer to leave it to others to detail the advantages of digital reading or the ecological benefits of paperless publishing. I'm much too attached to books for that. Ever since I learned to read, books, not electronic documents, have opened the world to me. Books were my companions, my roommates, my accomplices, my friends, and they remain so today. That I've actually succeeded in writing books is and remains the fulfillment of my wildest dreams.

Therefore, in *this* book, I would like to detail—without any claims to exhaustiveness—what I'd find myself missing if ever the book were to abandon me.

I don't pretend to unearth any heretofore unknown "pro-book" arguments. Rather, I'll devote myself to all the wonderful truisms with which I, and all of us in the culture of the book, live every day. All those attributes of the printed word may well be so familiar that you only fully recognize and appreciate them once they're gone.

THE BOOK, IN GENERAL

TAKING A BOOK in your hand, there's an utterly palpable sense of just how much doing, discussing, advising, and deciding has had to take place for it to exist at all.

Somebody wrote the text—perhaps even several somebodies, who pooled their labor and patched it together. Still others may have assisted them by way of research and travel. Agents scrutinized and submitted the manuscript, the publishing house's readers accepted it, costs were calculated, and the book's production proceeded. The text was proofread, and various corrections made. Once the paper mill delivered the material, a printing press printed it. The cloth for the cover originated in a weaving concern, glue and thread were supplied from elsewhere. Graphic designers created a dust jacket, the publisher's salespeople presented the book to the booksellers, the publicity department spread the word as widely as possible. Finally, drivers delivered the book to bookstores, and booksellers entered it into their inventory, displayed it on shelves, and sold it. And doubtless I've neglected many others who were conscious or unconscious parties to the process.

As a reader, one knows that not every text becomes a book; as far as literature is concerned, it's really only a very small portion. Those legendary mountains of unsolicited, unread manuscripts heaping the desks of literary editors are—to the chagrin of all authors whose texts languish unprinted—quite real. Thus every book marks an achievement for its text. Its very existence stands as evidence of the various hurdles it has had to clear.

And, therefore, books demand respect. Someone, somewhere in the world, is at this very moment full of pride as he presents his parents a copy of his first publication. Yet having done that, there arises the fear they won't read it, estranged from the imaginative world of their child, or of books in general. However, there's one thing that the great majority of parents will *certainly* do: place it respectfully on the living room bookshelf, conspicuous and always within reach, as proof to visitors, and above all to themselves, that their son or daughter has "made it." Building a house, conceiving or bearing a child, planting a tree, and writing a book—these are the accomplishments that prove one has lived to some purpose.

In the world of texts, books are the houses. They give their inhabitants shelter and protection, locate them, render them locatable and recognizable. Even now, from its sturdy house, the printed text gazes pityingly, perhaps even a bit condescendingly, out at its unprinted brothers and sisters floating free as manuscripts, typescripts, and computer files, roofless and subject to constant anxiety, destined to disappear without a trace.

Finally, a book is the embodiment of a complete, accomplished work, like the final bronze cast of a statue. Editing, printing, and binding have put an end to all labor on the text. From here on out, nothing more can be added, nothing deleted. There will have to be very good reasons for a "second, improved edition"—the hurdles are always high. And so, as a closed work, in millions and millions of copies, the book manifests the belief that all things important have a fixed form, a beginning, a middle, and an end.

As does, for example, a human life.

ON BODIES

THE NEW BOOK

A ONE-HUNDRED-YEAR-OLD text grows no younger when it is reprinted. Texts age, irrespective of their physical incarnations; only great art has the ability to suspend senescence. Nevertheless, a freshly appearing book that contains the hundred-year-old text is, undoubtedly, new. But *when*, exactly, is it new? At the moment it emerges from the printing press or the bindery? Or does it remain new as long as no one has read it? I'm not sure.

When it comes to paperbacks, it's often difficult to say whether it's new in the sense of not-having-been-read. Maybe a junior clerk at the bookstore has already secretly devoured it, warily turning the pages to leave behind no blemish, to leave the spine uncreased. With hardbacks on the other hand (or, at least, European hardbacks), it's simple to tell if a book is new, since most of them are shrink-wrapped in a thin plastic film—which every year seem to grow harder and harder to open without recourse to some sort of tool.

The hardback stands there wrapped in its plastic like some sealed comestible in airtight packaging—well-preserved, though somewhat lifeless and without aroma. Anyone given a shrink-wrapped book will immediately remove its plastic; no one who buys one for himself will add it to his bookshelf with the film intact. No, the book must be exposed to the air, even if, as with so many others, this first step sets it on the road to suffering.

Thus a new book is also a promise. It gives to its owner the sense that he's been granted a privilege. No matter how ancient the text, or how many times it has been reprinted, a new book presents itself in a state of virginity. If anything, it makes us feel that the whole previous history of its reading has been annulled, that we can begin again from scratch. As if even today we could open a copy of Shakespeare, Goethe, Zola, Joyce, etc., and return to the moment just after the author has laid down the quill or stepped away from the typewriter.

Naturally, this is a gimmick—one of those gimmicks without which our lives would be poorer. And new books have still further tricks up their sleeves—during their first readings at any rate. For instance, they open themselves automatically at precisely the place where one has paused in one's reading. As if the book's first reader has left behind a sort of trail, one he can pick back up again at any time. Or as if the book itself intends to preserve the trail of its very first reader.

New books smell new as well. What that actually means, however, varies. Back in the good old days they smelled good, like nature; in the bad old days they smelled bad, like cheap material. Nowadays they mostly smell like nothing at all, which corresponds to the dominant contemporary definition of a pleasant odor. So that smell is a gimmick as well, one that makes us believe the first reading of a new book is a kind of initiation, an absolutely first time.

At its worst, a book can seem so new that its owner hesitates to read it, or even feels repelled. Maybe he's afraid to smirch that pristine newness, not sure of receiving anything in return. Maybe, he thinks, the reading won't be anywhere near as cheerful, thrilling, inspiring, captivating, mysterious, as the newness of the book has promised. Maybe he'd better let the book lie unread, so as not to undermine his expectations, so as not to compromise that promise.

A hundred years ago, books arrived in the shops with their pages uncut. In a manner of speaking, one had to wound them in order to read them. There existed, expressly for this purpose, particularly flat and sharp knives. For thirty years now I've owned the first edition of one of Alfred Polgar's early books; it's called *Motion is Everything*. It was published in 1909, and its pages still remain uncut. A book so old, and definitively unread! Numerous times I've hefted the paper knife, but always I've set it aside again, unused. Because I wasn't quite sure that the book had been waiting for me to be its very first reader? Or because I wanted to put off still further the moment of that first reading? I don't know. In order to finally read the text, I borrowed another copy, and had it Xeroxed. For the time being, my own copy remains intact.

THE OLD BOOK

IN NINETY-NINE out of a hundred cases, an old book is a book that has been read numerous (if not innumerable) times. One can barely glance at it without beginning to reflect on its history—or at least on the fact that said history will probably never be known.

And yet antiquarian books are full of the traces of their past. There are various names in various scripts from various epochs—some of them, perhaps, crossed out by the volume's successive owners. There are bookplates that someone once glued to the flyleaf, and that someone else has attempted in vain to tear loose again. And, of course, the book's body will bear sundry signs of usage—and often one would be hard-put to say whether this resulted from a long series of measured perusals, or a single, rude, reckless reading.

To me personally, an old book conveys—with terrific force—that it has outlived one, two, or perhaps many owners. It bears an invisible dust jacket that proclaims: this is no mere consumer good. For every old book exists only because it wasn't thrown away after reading, nor after the deaths of its owners—because it was passed along to another reader. The old book is inherited, or gifted to a neighbor, or taken to an antiquarian bookshop, or bought up at an estate-sale or flea market. Perhaps it is donated along with other books to library or foundation, or exchanged for foreign specie in a wealthier neighboring country.

Certainly books are sometimes also used to light the oven, or simply tossed in the trash, and I daresay this probably happens more often than not. But in the best of situations, books are allowed to grow old like people or (these days) like horses. For decades now we've known how to recycle old paper—every day whole runs of newspapers are carted away and reprocessed. Yet we tend not to consider the reprocessing of books an ecological necessity. There are no recycling bins for books.

Plenty of people prefer old books to new as a matter of principle. Maybe because their age better conveys the value of the text; maybe because they favor the rare above the commonplace, above the welter of consumer goods. Or because they like to surround themselves with objects that seem to preserve a secret. Such people ensure that our society reserves a sanctuary for old books. I'll admit I'm unable to say whether or not this habit is alive or dying.

THE BIG BOOK AND THE LITTLE BOOK

WHEN FIRST they appeared, books were often so big and heavy that people were unable to hold them in their hands when they read. One had to lay them open on a table, or a lectern. Even today we say that someone "seats himself behind his book," when we want to say that someone is reading or studying with particular intensity.

So if books in their early years weren't portable property but big and heavy, this reinforces the quite correct impression that their contents weren't transportable as well, but rather the domain of a few rich and powerful individuals. Thus the book only truly came into its own, came to grips with its destiny when, with the advent of presses and moveable type, they grew smaller—finally so small that you could carry one around with you and read it anywhere. This convenient dissemination of various texts was the necessary precondition for the birth of modern science and the Enlightenment. All of which is to say: in the Western world, our culture's self-understanding is founded on the portable book. And the shape of a book, fitted in a steamer-trunk or in a jacket pocket, allowed its culture to be carried abroad to the farthest corners of the world.

Of course, there are still plenty of books that are fairly large and unwieldy, and visibly proud of it: atlases, for instance, enormous volumes of art or photographs, or so-called coffee table books, which (if nothing else) do yeoman's service as decorations. But, the undisputed champion among book formats is the modern paperback, which we've had with us since around 1900. They are small, light, affordable, and flexible, which is to say they present the fewest possible obstacles to the dissemination of their texts.

However, the paperback is still made of paper; it weighs something, takes up a certain amount of space. It can be damaged, or else misplaced. So one might say that it's quite logical that the next step in the dissemination of text would be to make that text's vehicle so "small" and "light" that it passes through an electric cable like the human voice. Considered from this perspective, the e-book is the ultimate fulfillment of Gutenberg's plan for the universal spread of writing.

Considered in *that* sense. But one can see, and should consider other senses as well.

THE BEAUTIFUL BOOK

REALLY, a book *shouldn't* be beautiful in the sense of being somehow decorated or adorned. It's better if its beauty arises exclusively from its printing—that is to say in a well-proportioned, readable typeface, and a sensible distribution of text on its pages. Its binding should be sober, unpretentious, naturally sturdy, though not too heavy. In these books the beauty emerges wholly from an air of functionality.

But in reality, there are other kinds of books as well. As a matter of fact, in German we've even adopted the technical term "Buchkunst" (not quite the same as "book-art"), a reference to how great the effort to achieve the "beautiful" book has been, and remains. Well and good—people design and decorate even modest every-day objects out of sheer joy in beautiful forms. And who'd say a word against that! We realize that, beyond nature, there are more than enough ugly things. Thus we have beautiful knives, and beautiful chairs, so that in the course of cutting or sitting one can enjoy, if you will, a kind of aesthetic surplus value.

Yet precisely this comparison exposes a distinction. The specific concepts of "knife-art" or "chair-art" don't really exist—they each fall under the category of "design." By "Buchkunst," however, I'm *not* referring to design, even where the latter's products aren't to my taste. I think that the relationship between books and art is much closer and more essential than that of chairs or knives.

The existence of Buchkunst strikes me more as an expression of respect for the text. You accentuate the latter's value by means of its apparel. One might be reluctant to release a text into the world naked, with no outer sign of its singularity, of the deference it deserves. A king doesn't show himself to the people in his underwear. And even a wholly modest garment like that of a priest or monk can signal dignity, even grandeur. Book-art is surely the art of creating a physical correlative for the spirit within.

In Buchkunst, as in all art, however, there lurks the risk of failure. I own quite a few books that I consider ugly. Many of them could be considerably improved by the removal of their dust jackets—but not all. Over-refined affectations like fancy headers, highly artificial typefaces or images imprinted on the edges of the pages annoy me greatly, since they suggest that someone believed the reader requires distractions from the text. But even the ugliest book is no argument against book-art. Just as little as a botched or silly piece of clothing is an argument for leaving the house without dressing. Nudity is not an alternative.

Nor is it with books.

THE DAMAGED BOOK

BOOKS CAN BE more or less knackered, put out of commission. Still, often enough even these remain legible. In other words, nothing irreversible has happened to the text, though damage may be everywhere evident as one reads. Water has rippled the pages and caused the color on their edges to smear and run. A tear runs obliquely through several pages—once it was probably patched with a strip of tape, long-since vanished, but which has left behind a brown rash. A flyleaf is missing, the binding is scuffed, and the spine hangs on a single strand of linen.

In this case one feels that the medium is, at the very least, a kind of message. The disorder is ubiquitous, unignorable, but the text behaves as if nothing has happened. It's as though one were hearing voices in the background; an alarming, unsettling noise. What has gone wrong here, you ask? Who's let his guard down, who's neglected his duty? Why was the book left lying in the water, the dust, the dirt, the sun? Who, exactly, was dealt a raw deal—a deal so raw that the book, in its turn, had to suffer?

When I read a damaged book, I concentrate on the text, trying to prevent its grim state from seizing me by the throat. If I succeed, surely the text itself should get the credit. And then, for that text, the sheer existence of the damaged book beneath the hand becomes a kind of distinction. Because, despite its condition, the book is still there. It hasn't been thrown away, or been used to light the oven, or torn up for scrap paper. Somebody, maybe even several somebodies, found its contents too important. And I am one of them.

To sum up: in the damaged book we see, on the one hand, how much the text depends on the book—and, on the other hand, how little.

THE INCOMPLETE BOOK

For several years I've been collecting the books of the Austrian author Peter Altenberg and have done so—how should I put it?—very ambitiously. Truth be told, my foolhardy goal was to assemble a copy of every one of Altenberg's fourteen books, in every edition, and in every binding. This harmless, though by no means inexpensive, mania possessed me completely—and in the '80s to boot, when one was forced to depend on antiquarians' catalogs and flea markets. Just how many volumes the "complete" collection would have contained I never exactly knew, since no catalog of all the editions existed. Maybe around a hundred? In any case, I'd gathered together about sixty different copies by the time I married and was forced to promise my wife that, at least in the matter of book-buying, I would be somewhat more restrained.

And I did, in fact, restrain myself. Yet one day, when the two of us were on vacation, I stumbled across a copy of Altenberg's very first publication, *How I See It*, in an antiquarian bookshop in Zürich—the very scarce first edition, whose price in those days generally topped three-hundred marks. Sadly, the book was no longer in its original condition. Probably first published in softcover, it was later re-bound, and somewhat severely trimmed. On the whole, however, it was definitely still a copy worth collecting. And—it was priced at thirty francs! At first I couldn't believe my luck; then I read the bookseller's little notice on the inside of the cover: *Missing last thirteen pages.*

I don't know how long I spent standing and brooding in that Swiss bookshop. Should I buy this book? Was it a reasonable or a completely unconscionable price? And most of all: is an incomplete book still a book at all, or merely a torso, a corpse?

In the end I bought it, but only so that later I wouldn't be able to reproach myself for leaving it behind. But I never liked it. I placed it on my shelf beside another copy of *How I See It*—which, though considerably less well-preserved (in fact, downright ratty), at least had all of its pages. Beside it, the incomplete copy looked, and looks, wretched. Once I attempted to replace the missing pages with photocopies. That only made things worse.

Today I feel much more certain: an incomplete book is a dead book. Or better say, a paper coffin for the text's cadaver. Others might see things differently. But I can't help myself. Unless, at some point in the near future, the thirteen missing pages of *How I See It* are offered to me separately, so that I can restore them to their rightful place, I think I will finally be capable of separating myself from this maimed copy. But how on earth could *that* happen?

It would probably be best if I sold the thing to someone as crazy as I am. Presuming, of course, such a person exists.

THE ANNOTATED BOOK

Usually, the signs that betray a previous reading are finger-marked pages, battered bindings, crooked spines, dog-eared corners or tattered book ribbons. But there are also readings that leave behind more distinct traces.

Once, as I was leaving the University Institute where I worked—this was some thirty years ago—I saw an old woman in the foyer, sitting on a folding chair. Before her on the floor lay a number of books; not many, maybe five or six. A depressing sight. Though I wanted to continue past at high speed, I paused, stood there looking, and took one of the books in my hand. It had, as they say, caught my eye. No wonder—it was a volume of poems by Stefan George, in the dark blue original edition designed by Melchior Lechter. The woman must have noticed my astonishment—maybe my air of cupidity as well. If I was interested in books like that, she said, I should come back to her house. She had plenty more.

So I followed her, curious, with the complicatedly mixed feelings of the collector, hoping to happen across a treasure and to acquire it on the cheap. We didn't have far to go: the woman lived in the city center, albeit in a rather tranquil neighborhood, one that seemed to have fallen a little out of step with time. As she led me into her basement, she explained that she suffered from a powerful forgetfulness. Thus the little notes stuck to the laundry bag, the provisions on the cellar shelves, and on the boxes of books. If I spent more than fifteen minutes in the basement, I might have to remind her how I'd come to be there in the first place. With that, she left me. Back then, I still didn't know what dementia was; so I took it as a comical aside and made my way over to the boxes.

After a couple of minutes, both hands were filled with books that I desperately wanted to buy; and a few moments later, they were empty again. The books, as the old lady had told me on our way over, had belonged to her husband. He had been born around 1900, had gone to college after the First World War, and become a teacher of German. Sadly, he hadn't long outlived his retirement. Now his widow had to care for a sick son, and needed to scrounge every cent she could find.

I had been thinking little or nothing while listening to this story. Now I sat on the cellar floor and felt like someone being justly punished for the sin of greed. The books were certainly those of a German teacher: that is to say, they'd been worked through with a sharp pencil, provided with extensive marginal commentaries, and would even have been perfectly suited for classroom use.

As an ambitious collector, I already had, in those days, some acquaintance with annotated books. Marginal notes and underlining with ballpoint or fountain pens were, of course, impossible to remove from paper; yet even writing in pencil had, often enough, proved unpleasantly durable. Hard lead pencils dragged furrows through thin and delicate paper, whereas lines in soft lead swelled out like ink when you attempted to rub them away. And then there were those so-called indelible pencils, which withstood every eraser. With a few exceptions, every attempt I'd made to liberate antiquarian books from commentary had ended in defeat. And here I was, facing my Waterloo.

Nonetheless, I remained a bit longer in the basement, albeit only to torture the collector in me. Among the German teacher's books were numerous works from notable authors active during the inter-war years, valuable first editions, like—it pains me to write it—Robert Musil's *The Man Without Qualities.* Yet all of these their owner had annotated with great meticulousness and a sharp pen. This meant, sad to say, that he had transformed them from valuable artifacts into the documentation of a busy professional life. Moreover, they had utterly lost their value—at least, for me.

In the end, all I took with me from the cellar was the volume of poems by Stefan George. Upstairs, the old woman remembered me, and we agreed on a price. Back at home I placed the book on my shelf, and never opened it again. I'm even afraid that my relationship with George may have suffered on account of this chance encounter.

ON USAGE

THE FAVORITE BOOK

USUALLY, when somebody asks you about your favorite book, what they mean is your favorite *text*. Nevertheless, what often comes to mind is a particular *book*, probably the one in whose shape that favorite was first encountered. For example, as a tremendous admirer of Theodor Fontane, I am sadly compelled, when asked this question, to remember an atrocious paperback edition of *Effie Briest.* It was a volume from a highly questionable collected edition of Fontane's work offered to readers shortly after the seventieth anniversary of his death for forty-nine marks, with horrible print on brownish paper and with utterly ludicrous pagination.

Or else I think of *Everything is Coco's Fault*, a children's book from the 1950s, from which I've long believed I remembered the following wonderful sentence: "Life consists of nothing so much as the beginnings of stories, which one has to tell right through to the end." When after almost fifty years I found myself again holding a copy of the book, I was terrifically moved. I remembered the cover illustration of the fiercely scowling ape, Coco, and the desperate children who were vainly attempting to catch him, and most of all the drawings, especially the maps of the story's various settings. I also believed I remembered that the sentence about the beginnings of stories had been in the middle of one of the right-hand pages. In fact, it didn't occur in the book at all. But what does that matter!

And then there's this: Gustav Schwab's *Gods and Heroes of Ancient Greece* is, for me, forever bound in the book-club edition in which I read it for the first time, and so many times afterward. A half-calf binding with covers shading from rust- to rosy-red, illustrated in the style of its time, and for me, back then, the epitome of elegance. How appropriate to its tales of honor, courage, and fortune. And how appropriate, also, to the vast amount of blood shed in the course of its text.

For a couple of hundred years it has been taken for granted that great texts are given their form as books—that is to say, three dimensions—so that they might be distinguished by the eyes and gripped by the hands. For many books the conjunction of form and content remains forever the same. Since my first encounter with it, I have read *Effie Briest* in various other editions, better in almost every respect. Yet for myself and its other readers, *Everything is Coco's Fault* exists in no other form than a grayish-beige half-cloth volume with its plain, naturalistic illustrations.

Through our daily experience we're so accustomed to identifying a text with a book that we tend to use the latter as a synonym for the former. Really, though, nobody ever writes a *book*; instead, one writes a *text*, which later, hopefully, will be published as a book. What's the difference! There's something to that false equivalence. For without its existence as a book, who knows whether the text would be something that would ultimately find its way into the world, could be apprehended, and taken to heart.

And thus one's favorite book is something like the book *par excellence*. Because here, at least, for the reader, text and physical form are self-evidently one. Spirit and substance are equivalent.

Which, incidentally, is always the case when something succeeds.

THE RIGHT BOOK

INSOFAR AS a book has a physical form, it supplants other objects from whatever spot in which it finds itself. Two books simply can't coexist in the same space. That sounds like a physical truism, but it's one that becomes painfully relevant when it's time to pack your backpack for a brief trip or your suitcase for a long vacation. Because in such situations there is space for only a limited number of books. Which means: one is forced to choose.

And not merely in the case of business trips or vacations. Just acquiring a book in the first place means making a (quite possibly painful) selection. Buying a book means bringing an object into the house for which space will have to be made, because two books simply can't... but you already know the rest. Bookshelves eventually fill. The stacks on the desk, night tables, and end tables grow until they tip and tumble. And if the space in the cellar and attic seems, at first, unlimited—believe me, it isn't!

The physicality of books leads to problems of transportation and furnishing that one is hard-put to solve. Beyond that, the book as a physical object stands as a symbol for the somber fact that we can read only a circumscribed number of books. Our lives, like our bookshelves, have a limited capacity. There are ways of attempting to calculate that capacity; they level out at an upper limit of around five thousand books, which you'll certainly only reach if you're a dedicated glutton for reading. Allowing for a book per week (and that isn't an insignificant amount!) sixty years of active reading would only amount to about three thousand books. Thus, what we'd be able to read if we really pushed ourselves could be accommodated on the walls of an average-sized room.

In other words: there's a certain correspondence between the amount of reading we can perform in a lifetime and the book-capacity of our living spaces. Apparently about as many texts enter our heads as books can fit into the average apartment, provided one makes space in said apartment for a library. Every new book we acquire takes up in our reading lives roughly the same amount of space as it does on our bookshelves.

Which is why one should always take care to select the *right* book.

THE WRONG BOOK

Often enough, the wrong book simply can't help it. Perhaps it was merely in the wrong place at the wrong time. Or we followed a bad recommendation, or didn't understand the recommendation correctly, or wrote it down *in*correctly. In any case: the wrong book is an irritation, one that you'd gladly get rid of. Yet as a physical object, it asserts its presence; it isn't so simple to remove this mistake from your world.

Of course, you can try. For example, by putting the wrong book in a holding pattern on the nightstand. Perhaps the eye's familiarity with the wrong book will eventually convert it to the right one. Or you can inter it in a bookcase, so that time will accomplish the same feat unaided. On the other hand, you can take action and give the book away, or lend it to someone, ridding yourself of the memory of the error.

Wrong books are especially bad when they supplant right books. Unfortunately this happens frequently on trips or during vacations, especially on so-called (or actual) deserted islands. There, the right book is, for a while at least, inaccessible, and immediately the wrong book becomes (for hours, days, or weeks) a painful reminder that you've (yet again) played fast and loose with your limited time for reading and living. And then the wrong book may well become the focus of all the rage that all the wrong things in this world have nourished in us. Woe to the wrong book in such cases!

I personally believe that there exists a perfectly good procedure for making a right book out of a wrong one when you happen to be sitting on the aforementioned island. You have to read it. Maybe it was, in fact, simply a good book in disguise. And even if it turns out to have been a genuine wrong book, then at least you've read a book you might have otherwise overlooked. And this experience might possibly be more rewarding than having read the upteenth book that suits your taste.

THE EXPENSIVE BOOK AND THE CHEAP BOOK

THE SIZE of the buyer's wallet generally decides whether a book is expensive or cheap. Cheap and expensive are relative categories. Looking back at their history, books were at first so expensive that, for most people, they were all but unattainable; then, over time, they grew cheaper. The ideal ratio between the average price of a new book and the average buying power of the average European prevailed, so I once heard, about forty years ago. But in my opinion, this is based on a false calculation—books are clearly less expensive today than ever before, since one can buy such an enormous number of them (which are not necessarily even used) so cheaply.

Nonetheless, I'm sure that even today every reader could tell the story of a book that was expensive, very expensive, perhaps too expensive. In my case, it's the story of the luxury volume *The Great Age of Sail*, a translation from the French that the German publishing house of Delius Klasing first added to its catalog in 1970, and who maintained it there for over twenty years.

It was in that year, 1970, when my enthusiasm for old sailing ships had just begun, that I walked into a bookstore and asked what they might have on this subject over and above what was available in my local public library. The answer was: nothing. The likely shelves offered no more than guidebooks for amateur sailors and a volume on the beauty of the Norwegian fjords. But the bookseller had an idea. Clearly it hadn't been long since the representative of Delius Klasing had visited the store—and so I was able to glance through the catalog of that press's new releases. No question about it, *The Great Age of Sail* was precisely the book I was looking for. Richly illustrated in full color, with fold-out plates containing cross-sections of ships and diagrams of rigging. A must-have in every sense.

But it cost fifty-four marks! I'll leave it to experts to compute what that would come out to today. That result wouldn't be as important as a very particular number was back then, a number I knew only too well: five! I received five marks of pocket money per month, to which I was able to add a bit scrounged here and there from my (sadly few) relatives. This meant that, as a rule, I could usually scrape together as much as a ten-spot; but a book priced at fifty-four marks was entirely out of my league.

Today, as I write this, the book is lying beside me. The price is still marked, along with the ISBN, on the flyleaf. Beneath it is the bookplate that I designed myself back around 1980, and an autograph from the present publisher, Konrad Delius, which I asked for in 2007. Back in 1970, as I pondered whether or not to order the book, Delius was still a schoolboy, just like me.

From all of which it should be obvious that I did, in fact, order and buy the book. Yet to my own surprise, I'm no longer able to say how I managed to find the money. Not a trace of the memory remains. I'm sure I didn't steal it, but what I *did* do to assemble the sum—I simply don't know. Perhaps—no, *certainly*—I begged, lied, and dissembled to such an extravagant degree that shame has extinguished the memory. But never mind that: the main thing is that I managed to buy the book.

And how I've adored it! Reading it has always been like an act of worship. Unfolding the color plates—taking care not to crease them, of course—was a ritual. Though I once believed firmly that my books should stand on the shelves without dust jackets, I never actually discarded *Great Age*'s jacket, and for a long time now the two have been reunited. While it was uncovered, the book's spine grew somewhat faded, its edges a little dusty-grey. But that doesn't matter. Whenever I take the book in my hands, I physically experience the older and so much lovelier meaning of the expression: "This is *dear* to me."

But it is only to me that this book still seems "dear." Though its illustrations have lost none of their beauty, its text none of its substance, it has, however, shed almost all of its material value. On the internet it would fetch about four Euros, that is to say not even the price of a pack of cigarettes; back when the book was new, those same cigarettes would have cost two marks.

As I've already said: with their greater availability, books have become, in general, cheaper. This should be welcomed; it's in the economic interest of the reader. But I fear that the aura around the book will suffer because of it. After all, there are already ideas in circulation like the "cultural flat-rate" and the universal freedom of all cultural artifacts. At the beginning I wrote that every book conveys a sense of the hurdles its text had to clear to make its appearance in print. To me, back then, as a thirteen-year-old boy, the enormous price of *Great Age* made absolutely clear to me how much work would be required before I could immerse myself in it, pore over its images, unfold its diagrams. That was a good lesson to learn. I don't know whether we can do without it.

THE DISCOVERED BOOK

In recent years, my method of buying books has become almost frighteningly pragmatic. I'm probably not the only one moving in this direction. More and more people are buying books through the internet, and anyone who takes this approach generally knows ahead of time exactly what he's looking for. In most cases everything goes simply and smoothly. Meanwhile, small bookstores are dying one after another—stores whose great merit has always been to provide people with books whose titles they *don't* know, or else to help them pick out a volume appropriate for their niece or to take on vacation to Ibiza.

One remaining refuge for the wandering bibliophile (I hereby establish this technical term) is the flea market. Here, one can't really ask after particular writers or titles, and only seldom will there be shelves organized by subject, or even arranged alphabetically by author. Nor will one find featured the season's bestsellers. Instead, you find boxes brimming with a hodgepodge of everything, and you have to bend and contort yourself to see what's inside.

For years I spent almost every weekend seeking out flea markets, setting my sights on the bookstands alone. I've taken and weighed thousands of books in my hands, bought hundreds of them, sometimes delighted at my find, sometimes purchasing halfheartedly, sometimes taking a vague shot in the dark. There have been books fantastically suited to my collection, and also those that necessitated the opening of a *new* collection. Like any longtime lottery player, I've had a couple of lucky hits—that is to say, rare and valuable books I've been able to obtain for precious little. Among them were first editions of Franz Kafka and Robert Walser. Sadly, I've had to re-sell most of these books to finance my ongoing passion for collecting.

Rummaging around for books can itself easily become an obsession. I certainly found this to be the case. And said obsession was constantly threatening to make me poor. But I always scoffed at the idea that it might make me sick to boot. Yet the physical challenges can't be denied. I'd rise early in the morning on flea market days, drink a quick cup of coffee and eat nothing. I was already so wide awake, so nervous. Hours later my hands would be filthy, my back aching, and I would have acquired a couple of books whose very existence I'd never imagined. For instance, I first made the acquaintance of the crime reporter Sling (a pseudonym for Paul Schlesinger) at the flea market, and likewise the feuilletonist Walther Kiaulehn. In the evening I'd sit in my room, completely exhausted, with my new books and a bottle of beer. Most of the time I was very happy.

And I asked myself: had I actually chosen these books? Or had they chosen me? Sometimes I felt that they had. Maybe for decades they'd been plotting their positions, so as to cross my path on this particular Saturday morning in Krefeld-Fischeln or wherever. Could it really have been sheer chance? Or was it a species of fate, as with two people who follow winding paths to meet each other, and afterwards spend their lives together?

Sure, I know. It's probably a beautiful illusion. If I'd encountered different books, I would have bought them. But the seeker of books lives by the illusion that between him and his discoveries a different relationship obtains than that between customer and merchandise. With seekers of books at the flea market, it isn't a question of precise needs and specific satisfactions, like buying something on the internet. To come right to the point, it's more a question of the auspicious moment, and the unexpected, the inevitable, but fateful, encounter.

THE GIFTED BOOK

"A BOOK IS A GIFT." For a long time this was the advertising slogan of... I'm not sure who—maybe the German Publishers' and Booksellers' Association? Quite possibly. But in any case: to this very day I continue to stumble across this little pronouncement. What does it actually mean? That, when in doubt, a book is a gift you really can't go wrong with? Or is it that a book is the *ideal* gift? Or maybe even that *every* book is, per se, a gift (to humankind)?

Whatever it may be, the slogan contains a truth as banal as it is economically relevant: books are gifts to the extent that many of them are bought precisely to *serve as* gifts. And for that purpose they are indeed outstandingly suited. Books are the perfect size, neither too big nor too small, they have the right price, neither too measly nor too extravagant, and furthermore they can be tastefully wrapped with little effort.

Indeed, anyone who gives a book isn't risking terribly much. In most circles, presenting a book is seen as a praiseworthy, or at least uncriticizable act. For a graduation, a confirmation, a birthday, for an anniversary, you receive from your headmaster, your father, your friend: a book. Not a blanket, not a skateboard, not a salami. Generally speaking, a book will work smoothly as a gift even if the giver knows nothing about it, and the recipient is never going to read it. Hardly anybody with any manners will protest aloud if he receives the coffee table book *Venice in Winter*, though he has no particular relationship either to the one or the other. Refusing the gift of a book simply isn't done.

Moreover, it's a kind of commonplace that accepting a book doesn't commit the receiver to reading it. With a book, one extends an option, but doesn't exert pressure. And finally, it's easy to discreetly deal with the gift of an unwanted book. One simply sticks it onto the shelf beside the others. It will look perfectly comfortable there, as if it's waiting patiently for its turn to be read. You can also exchange it for another with no problem whatsoever. Or you can simply re-gift it.

Then again, the gift of a book can open all kinds of opportunities, transmit a whole plethora of (secret) messages to the recipient. Books can be declarations of love, or invitations to a community of minds. When you give a rose-grower a book on roses, you pay obeisance to his mania (one rarely encountered in everyday life). When you give him a book on orchids, you're making an appeal to his cosmopolitanism. The gift of a book can serve as a reminder of common experiences, or stand as an attempt to share with the receiver the powerful emotions that one felt oneself reading the book.

I don't know what percentage of all books are bought as gifts. The proportion, they say, is high. Very high. As an author, I don't really care to know. Who wants to think that, of all the books he sells, a good number will be given, but never read? After all, there are such things as gift-books—that is, books that were specifically designed and published for the sole purpose of being given.

But no hard words about the gifted book! If from one day to the next we struck the book from the list of appropriate gifts and accorded the giving of books the same social and cultural significance as the giving of, let's say, condoms or shoe inserts, the whole industry would suffer a terrible slump. Publishing houses would close, and it wouldn't be only the authors of gift-books who would find themselves out of work.

And what's more, the whole world of gift-giving would be deprived of its best means of reducing the level of embarrassment to the minimum. The strain to the psyche around the holidays would rise dramatically, the prevailing mood of depression would increase, and as a consequence the gross national product would plummet. It doesn't bear contemplating! So please, never forget: "A book is a gift."

THE SIGNED BOOK

After the reading at the cultural center, a long line stretches before the author seated at the table. The novices at this ritual have just purchased the author's book at the stand run by the local bookshop and are now fairly nervous. What if the author speaks to them? What if he asks to whom, exactly, he should sign the book? What can you say without making yourself ridiculous?

The professionals are anything *but* nervous. They've brought their entire collection of the author's works with them from home. Standing in line, most of them are already holding their books open to the appropriate page. And even before the signer can spring the question, they're ready with their particular wishes, for instance: "Please, just the name and date, no need to add the place. And with this pen, if you don't mind!"

Naturally, the author has been asked beforehand by the moderator if he'd be willing to sign his books in connection with the reading; he has kindly agreed. What else could he say without making himself impossible?

When for the first time I signed one of my own books for an audience member previously unknown to me (March 18th, 1991, Frankfurt-am-Main, the Kohl Bookstore, of blessed memory), I was nearly bursting with pride. Because I knew well enough what it meant: a signed book! For years I myself had collected not merely rare books, but (the better to ruin myself financially) signed ones as well. Or, to put it more accurately: *attempted* to collect, since the offerings in the antiquarian catalogs were pricey and scarcely any signed copies found their way into the flea markets; the sieves of the rare-book sellers were growing ever finer.

The crown jewels of my collection were (and are to this day) a first edition of Peter Altenberg's *How I See It* with a long handwritten dedication by the author to an unknown woman, and a copy of Karl Kraus's Altenberg anthology that he had inscribed to Mary Dobržensky, a patroness of Rainer Maria Rilke. How I managed to finance the purchase of these books is a story in itself. I only mention all this here in order to demonstrate that even on March 18th, 1991, I believed I understood why someone would want to possess a scrap of an author's handwriting.

Yet now, much later, after having signed so many other books, I've begun to ask myself: do I *really* know?

Sure, a signed book is, to begin with, an acknowledged collector's item; one can buy it from antique dealers along with similar things like postage-stamps, lithographic postcards of cities, or little elephants and lions made of silver. As the fame of the author increases, so does the value of the signed book, and people can speculate on this possibility with great success. If you can get it signed by the author after a reading, you've acquired it for no more than the retail price, and with a pleasant memory to boot.

For example, I own a copy of Peter Bichsel's small prose volume *Actually, Frau Blum Would Really Like to*

Meet the Milkman (10th printing of the revised 1974 edition). After one of Bichsel's readings in my hometown, I told him that his story "The Animal Lover," included in that book, had been the assigned text for my final exam in high-school German. Bichsel, misunderstanding my intention in mentioning it, wrote an apology in my book. In fact, my interpretation of the piece received a high grade and was among the major reasons I decided to go on and study literature in college. But with the long line at my back, I hardly had the chance to explain this to Bichsel. Despite—or rather, *because* of—this misunderstanding, the little book remains for me a lovely *aide-de-memoire*.

But maybe the signed book isn't merely another addition to the book collection, or an object to stir up memories. Could it be that it's hiding something deeper? Where books are concerned, my rule of thumb is: when in doubt, the answer is *yes*.

Up until the advent of printed books some five hundred years ago, books were written by hand. Every one of them was an original; unique and recognizable. Since Gutenberg, however, books have been widely distributed in vast, identical editions. Perhaps one could say that there persists a sharp longing for that lost unity of text and handwriting? Is that possible? After all, the first printed letters imitated the handwriting of the medieval scribes in order to improve the new medium's acceptance among readers. And maybe, five hundred years later, we still haven't quite gotten over the fact that, through the printing and mass replication of books, the text has been distanced from its author and, thereby, shed its aura of individuality. The manuscripts of important texts are housed in archives and museums and exhibited like relics; literary scholars continually pore over them in the hope of uncovering something about them lost in their transition to print.

Thus, the readings at the cultural center might just have the goal of slaking the reader's desire for aura, for singularity. The presence of the author—his voice, probably identical with the voice in his head that silently spoke the text for the first time; and finally, his handwriting on the endpaper or title page of the book, the opportunity to take it home and preserve it. It might be that all of this is a trick. But it works. By means of the signature, the mass-produced book is transformed, at least symbolically, back into the unique specimen that its text, despite its multiplications, has always been, and remains.

THE PERSONALIZED BOOK

In the course of my flea market trips I'm continually coming across books that somebody has, in one way or another, put his personal stamp on. For lack of a better way of explaining, I'll give an example: on the flyleaf of a book by Hans Carossa, I found written: "My dearest Walter, in grateful remembrance of April 19th, 1959, from your Elisabeth." Only a couple of words in a book, nothing to interfere with one's reading—and yet!

Holding such a book in my hands, I know I am unquestionably in possession of a kind of artifact, a record of the circumstances, dreams, and intentions of people like Walter and Elisabeth, about whom I'll never learn anything more, and who I'll never meet. And I think: here two people have managed to bind a particular day, a promise or a kiss, so closely to a book, perhaps even in a text, that they've actually created a unity lasting for decades—a book that has survived the individuals involved, just as it has their vows and kisses.

Often enough, it's no more than a name and a date on the flyleaf or title page. Here someone has declared their title of ownership. Such behavior may well strike the book's subsequent owner almost as vandalism; but the inscriber ought to be forgiven, since it wasn't really *his* idea—he was simply following an old tradition.

Because in earlier times books were so rare and expensive, names were commonly inscribed, or bookplates were inserted to guard against theft or loss, or at least to increase the chances that, in the wake of theft or loss, they might be identified and retrieved. And even in an age where books aren't so expensive (if not actually *cheap*), marks of ownership remain sensible, since massive numbers of books are still left lying around, or lent out, or forgotten, or lost.

And indeed, maybe by writing his name and the date on the title page, a book's owner is merely asserting the reader's role in the game. He is, to a certain extent, signaling the successful completion of that act of communication we call "the book." When his hand lifts the pen to inscribe his signature, he seems to declare that the circuit has at last been closed. Author: Thomas Mann. Text: *The Magic Mountain.* Reader: Wilfried Schumacher, began reading July 23, 1981.

Thus the owner's inscription is saying two different things. First of all: *Hands off of this book!* Or: *Return to owner!* At the same time he's confirming, with signature and date, that *this* copy, at least, has fulfilled its purpose. It has managed to cross paths with a real, breathing reader. The whole damned struggle was not in vain.

THE LOANED BOOK

AT THE RISK of repeating something already well known: you don't have to own a book in order to read it. In some respects, books are a kind of common property. And that doesn't hold true just for library books. Even when privately held, books have an exceptional status. Long before one borrows an acquaintance's porcelain dinner plates or lawn mower, one will have asked him ten times for a book. (Unless they're collectors' items!) Plates and mowers are in a certain sense more intimate possessions than books. And it's understood (if only tacitly) that only the book's paper, and not its text, can be possessed by its owner. What's more, you flatter a book's owner if you make their choice of books your own.

Nonetheless, the lending and borrowing of books is an extremely prickly affair. The porcelain dishes may be needed for a first communion, the mower because one's own is in the shop. Thus, when lending them, one can set a firm deadline for their return. With books, it's a different story. Because reading is no family party or yard work. It's far more prone to deferral or interruption; it can last for ages or founder for the moment. Which is why the lender usually says: "No hurry! Give it back to me once you've read it."

This is well-meant. But afterward, fate takes its course. If the borrower puts it on the back burner, even for a little while, the book lies heavy on his soul. An internal clock begins its imperious ticking: *You're going to have to return the book.* On the other hand, the borrower certainly doesn't want to rush, to let himself rush, through a book. Where would we be if we let that happen! Giving the book back unread is no solution either. In the first place, the borrower would probably have to admit he'd requested the book for no reason, and in the second, it would surely make him look like a fusspot. And the lender is in a fix as well. He may be terrifically irritated by the delay, but nevertheless deliberately resists asking for his book, so as not to come off as a fusspot himself. After all, he himself said: "No hurry!"

Many loaned books spend weeks, months, even years, in the limbo of *still-not*. Still not read, but soon. Still not returned, damn it, but not long now. I promise. In the worst cases, the loaned book becomes completely unreadable for the borrower. What's more, he prefers to remove the thing from his sight, lest it remind him of his predicament. Possibly it will be packed in a moving box and leave the city, the country, the continent; and finally, whether in the worst kind of bad circumstances, or out of sheer forgetfulness, the borrower will wind up counting it among his own possessions. Still later, the book will have outlived both lender and borrower. But only when it finds itself purchased again, most likely for a few cents at a flea market, will its stain, its stigma, be obliterated. Now, at last, it can be read again.

Until someone borrows it.

THE VANISHED BOOK

Because books are physical objects, they're prone to getting lost. They especially like to do this on the road, an event that can ruin a trip. At any rate, I'm rarely as desperate as when the Intercity Express begins to pull out of the station, and I realize that I've left my book behind on the local train. Suddenly, I find myself menaced by that most terrible, and most unshakeable, of all traveling companions: boredom. And without fail, the trip becomes, at the very least, three or four times longer than I'd anticipated.

Books go missing at home as well, and more often then not, right in the place where they actually belong—that is, the bookshelf. The ampler one's household collection of books, the greater the chance that a particular book will wind up in the wrong place. And ever since Edgar Allan Poe's story "The Purloined Letter," we know that a sheet of paper is never more completely hidden than when it's among other papers.

The problem of lost books is correspondingly graver in large libraries. At least once a year during the years I worked at the university, I was involved with the ongoing review of that institution's library. It was my rather straightforward task to bring the call numbers of the non-circulating collection back into order. Every time I went to work, it turned out that not only were books missing, but there were hundreds of volumes completely out of place. We all knew why: students had shifted books around, so as to permanently keep them all to themselves. An entirely understandable, though nonetheless reprehensible act.

A vanished book can do more than ruin a traveler's mood: it can actually get said traveler into a fix. Suddenly one's preparatory materials for the seminar are unavailable, the notebook containing formulae and figures for the presentation has been misplaced, the cookbook with the recipe for this evening's dinner is nowhere to be found—and you're already in hot water. A replacement for the lost book isn't so easy—indeed, it may be impossible.

Quite apart from the private emotion, there's a collective fear of losing books as well; and this is so powerful that the disappearance of books ranks high among the great cautionary myths. So we see that the loss of library collections has become a great metaphor for the loss of culture. With the loss of the Alexandrian Library went the wisdom of the ancients. And how much literature draws for its subject on missing books! I'll merely mention Umberto Eco's novel, *The Name of the Rose.*

I think that this anxiety over the possible loss of books confirms our sorry certainty that the achievements of culture are neither universal nor altogether secure. On the contrary, they are tied to particular bearers, and share their respective fates, so that in the very worst cases nothing of them remains behind. There might be a collective memory, but it's full of holes, and in no way immune to forgetfulness. The mind requires a vessel to protect it, just as the text requires a book. Better still: *books*, so that if one is lost or destroyed, another can replace it.

THE STOLEN BOOK

Back at the beginning of my college years, stealing books from the bookstore was considered a kind of rite of passage for individuals of independent mind. In certain circles, texts were seen as public property. The fact that they existed in the actual, everyday world, for the most part, as commodities and private possessions—that is, as books—was considered a strategy of domination on the part of the capitalist system, one that ought to be met whenever possible by acts of insubordination, even vandalism.

Back then I did, in fact, steal a single book. It was a completely gratuitous act, a test of courage that one would associate with a pubescent boy—and immensely more stupid because it was delayed till my early twenties. My object was a copy of Klaus Mann's novel *Mephisto*, which after a long prohibition had only just been republished under murky legal circumstances. It struck me as a fine quarry, especially given that copies were stacked in a huge pile by the doors of the bookstore.

Though the theft was successful, it caused me tremendous distress. I read the book immediately, in hopes that the reading might atone for the crime. Of course, that was nonsense. I also went back to purchase another copy, let them give me a receipt, and on exiting left the stolen book behind on the scarcely diminished pile, thereby ending my flirtation with the actionist critique of capitalism.

Later, during my years as a collector, I was time and again getting myself into situations in which I was forced seriously to think about theft. So many books seemed to belong on my shelves, among my other volumes (and nowhere else!), that breaking the law frequently struck me as warranted. The conditions of their current ownership felt terribly unjust, though not from broad social or political considerations, but rather because my personal right to the book clearly seemed to me more substantial and profound than that of this particular antiquarian or public library. Only once did my desire actually prove stronger than my fear of being caught. But wild horses couldn't drag out the details of that particular incident.

The book thief is an attractive, though also ambivalent, figure. On the one hand, he takes from others. That simply can't be condoned—where would it lead? On the other hand, he's an intellectual among thieves, a Robin Hood in the world of the mind. One wishes that there could be established in the world of books legal relationships other than those of consumer goods, and ideally they would be those that apportioned books according to the genuine needs and inner qualities of readers. Though it's difficult to imagine how something like *that* might happen.

However, since becoming an author myself, I've lost almost all of my romantic feelings for the book thief. Anyone who steals my books thinks little of my work, or enriches himself by way of it, and thereby diminishes my earnings. Over the course of several centuries we have developed an economic-cultural system in which there's at least some chance an author can support himself by means of his pen. Without the concept and law of "intellectual property," it would be completely impossible, and therefore it ought to remain in practice. And it only functions if the theft of intellectual property—in whatever form it exists—is prohibited.

At the same time, the book itself functions in at least some sense as an anti-theft device. Though it can't unfailingly protect a text from theft and plagiarism, by giving the text an official, authorized form, it can at least make that theft much more easily identified. At the beginning of this book, I said: in the world of the text, books are houses. I should have expanded: they are both house and identification card. They clarify ownership and vouch for the authentic form.

Nonetheless, there are still cases of text-theft, despite all legal regulations. The most spectacular recent case was that of the Berlin students who, in 1970, produced a pirate edition of Arno Schmidt's novel, *Bottom's Dream*. As often in that period, the dissemination of the text was widely touted as a social act; while the original edition cost over three-hundred marks, the pirate edition was available for a mere hundred. But truly the act was anything *but* social, since it jeopardized the earnings of an author living in precarious circumstances. And the pirate edition lowered the sales prospects for a later, official edition of the book.

An unspectacular variety of pirate edition is the fully or partly photocopied book, which is taken quite for granted in everyday student life. A German foundation is at least trying, by setting up a fund through donations from the manufacturers and installers of copy-machines, to compensate authors for these photocopies of their work. But with continual technical advances it is becoming harder and harder to control acts of duplication. With the smartphone, almost everyone now carries a pirating machine in his pocket. And I don't even want to talk about how difficult it is to protect digital texts, how ubiquitous they are, and how easy they are to steal.

THE BOOK LEFT BEHIND

In the vacation home that we've been renting for the past fifteen years stands an enormous cupboard. Though it's intended to house glasses and crockery, over time it has also accumulated books brought along and left behind by holiday guests. Over the years we have ourselves, in no small measure, contributed to enlarging this collection. Thus far I've made my way through some half-dozen books from this accidental library, entirely at random, and every one of them books that otherwise would never have found a place on my reading list. To take two examples: a biography of Admiral Canaris, German spy and member of the resistance, and Eric Malpass's *Morning's at Seven*, a book I had read as a child, but had completely forgotten about.

I've been told that back in the days of passenger ships, and especially aboard smaller ones, the ship's library would largely consist of the leavings of previous travelers. If on disembarking you hadn't yet finished a book from the collection, you were permitted to take it along with you, provided you left another one behind. As if on their own, these on-board libraries would have regularly filled up with titles representing, as we'd say today, the international mainstream.

In my experience, one doesn't find books left behind these days in the rooms of hotels or pensions. I fear that they are being disposed of by the staff on (as the expression goes) hygienic grounds. One exception to this is the rooms of guesthouses or writers' residences, for instance the Literary Colloquium at Wannsee in Berlin. Nowadays such guest quarters house—whether for short- or long-term stays—people who read less for purposes of sheer entertainment. Which also means that they read books which, in the main, aren't simply left behind, but rather gathered together around one at home. When such people do in fact separate themselves from books by leaving them behind, mustn't that mean that they're expressing a literary indictment?

I've always asked myself this question when putting up for the night at Wannsee. The gatherings of books in the rooms were always highly heterogeneous, far removed from both the mainstream bestsellers and the critics' seasonal darlings. And every time I was downright horrified by all of the authors and titles I didn't recognize, indeed, of whom I'd never even heard.

I'll admit that I've never gotten engrossed in a title taken from such a guest-house library. But they certainly foster humility. "There are," they seem to say, "more books between heaven and earth than are dreamt of in your philosophy, my dear." The universe of books is enormous, and continually expanding. For every known, treasured, highly praised, hyped, and filmed book there are dozens, hundreds, leading tranquil, perhaps even silent and invisible lives. There are books that you'll never encounter if you don't know about them, if you don't seek them out. Unless, that is, you happen to spend a sleepless night in the appropriate guest room.

THE DISCARDED BOOK

For almost fifteen years I had at my disposal a basement that, to be honest, I didn't really need. It could just as well have remained empty. But it didn't. Instead, I began to fill it with objects I didn't want to throw or give away, despite no longer having any use for them. And there's more. This basement always gave me the courage—indeed, practically seduced me—to haul things into the house, to begin collections that I wasn't entirely convinced my heart was in. No problem! said the basement. In case my enthusiasm ever flagged, it could quickly absorb it all and relieve me. Out of sight, out of mind. So it went, and over the course of the years the basement was filled to the brim.

Naturally, books wound up being stored there as well. Whenever a shelf in my living-room or office grew too full, I'd take a few books to the basement: some that I'd read, but didn't absolutely need to have around me, others that I assumed I wasn't going to read anytime soon, or possibly not at all. Over time, all the textbooks from my student days, business books I'd reviewed for a magazine, antiquarian mispurchases, duplicate copies, review copies, and failed gifts found their way there. In the end, the scope of this so-to-speak negative collection added up to around three Ikea Billys (the standard measurement for one's private stock of books).

Now, I'd certainly never, for the life of me, conceived that there might be something else to do with these books than to store them away in the basement, that more-or-less well-managed animal sanctuary for worn-out or incongruous objects. Therefore, I accepted the idea that, over the years, the basement would become a dangerously melancholy place. It happened that for weeks at a time I'd avoid it, dreading the confrontation with so many disappointments and mistakes. Who'd willingly visit a well-sorted museum of his own failures?

Then, one September 11th, the water arrived. Not from above, but from below; the house's groundwater-pump malfunctioned, flooding the basement on a dry day, for no reason whatsoever. Quite democratically, it got hold of a little bit of everything—including, of course, the lower rungs of my bookcases, on which were several boxes of new arrivals, still waiting to be sorted.

Under normal circumstances I would have been simply furious. It's possible that the damage suffered by that unhappy collection of books might even have brought about my reconciliation with these exiles. But scarcely a week before the flood my wife and I had decided to move, and since then I'd known I was going to have to part with the lion's share of my basement stock.

Why am I telling you all of this? In order to excuse myself—or, better, in order to attempt to minimize my guilt through narrative. For, indeed, Your Honor, I admit it: a few weeks after the flooding, I threw away some of the books housed in the basement. In other words, I began to kill off the occupants of my sanctuary.

Not that this was at all easy for me. Even discarding

the drenched and slightly moldy volumes was painful. I was honestly grateful for their condition, which supplied at least some excuse for my conduct. Throwing away the undamaged books, on the other hand, struck me as pure sacrilege.

Now, I'm capable of rattling off at any time the grounds for my exoneration: an antiquarian had declined (though with thanks) the collection when I offered it to him—at any price. Textbooks from the '70s and '80s, according to him, were good for nothing but scrap paper. Reached by phone, the supervisor of a neighborhood library barely let me get a word in: "Thank you kindly, but we don't take donations of books more than four years old." And even the local animal shelter, which organized a regular charity sale, was only interested in children's books and mystery novels. What's more, our move was imminent, and what with the process of disassembling this and that, I had neither the time nor leisure to provide the books with new owners.

Still, Your Honor, I know that just by the tone of my excuses you recognize their emptiness. You don't abandon animals, even when they bite or grow terribly annoying. And you don't throw books away. *Basta*! When you can't keep them, animals or books, you have to come up with some solution. We owe them—our whole culture owes them—that much. And I sinned against them, when at last I hired a junk-removal man, the knacker of the book world.

But it got even worse. Toward the end of the liquidation and the move, when the deed had already been done, I discovered in an area of the basement that had somehow remained dry, two boxes I didn't recognize at all, filled with books. Not desensitized by my crime, but rather roused to action, I had an idea: I placed a bookshelf in the lobby of our parish church, filled it with the books, a crude mixture of all possible genres, and tacked up a little card describing their circumstances.

A month later I came back to fetch the shelf. It was empty. Completely empty. And I felt even worse than before. There might have been a way!

Your Honor, I beg for a lenient sentence.

THE FORBIDDEN BOOK

As long as one only needs to track down and destroy all of the books housing a certain text in order to suppress it, there is at least a theoretical chance of success. If, for example, an edition hasn't yet been shipped, and thus distributed through the world, one could confiscate and shred it. If you could get hold of all manuscript copies, you would effectively smother the text, at least for the time being. But the novel *Fahrenheit 451* offers a lovely parable about how difficult, if not impossible, such initiatives have always been, and remain, to accomplish in practical terms. In a future dictatorship, all books without exception are forbidden; so people have learned the great texts by heart in order to preserve them.

There are plenty of stories from dictatorships past and present about forbidden texts and books. How manuscripts are smuggled via tricks and circuitous routes into other countries, and then, as books, smuggled back in. How they're fitted with different covers and bindings in order to hoodwink the authorities. And also how the possession of a forbidden book can change, or end, a life.

In our democracies, whose basic political concepts rely on freedom of expression, the banning of books is a kind of acid test, showing how seriously the authorities take the liberty of words. Trials over the banning of a book, no matter what the reason or on whose behalf, always arouse tremendous attention since they represent the conflict between two competing interests: on the one hand freedom, on the other hand safety and security. One person wants to say what he wants to say; somebody else wants to remain unidentified in the work, or else the State believes that the citizens must be protected from its contents. In addition to the specific case, such trials address the fundamental question at issue: which way the scales tip in cases of doubt, towards the protection of the community or the freedom of the individual.

Thus trials over banning books are inevitably distressing. They turn into an airing of dirty laundry, experts tweezing paragraphs from texts, jurists agonizing over philosophical dilemmas. All the same, we have to live with such trials—we should even be grateful for them. Because in them arise concrete examples of what will increasingly determine the everyday life and future of our democracies: the conflict, never wholly resolved, between the necessities of security and the privilege of freedom.

THE MISTREATED BOOK

A "Bible bump" has nothing to do with religion—it's a colloquial term for a subcutaneous cyst generally occurring in the vicinity of a joint, and filled with a sort of gelatinous substance. One traditional way of removing such a growth was to take a heavy book, for example a Bible, and use it to slam the affected area. Note that one didn't use a board or a hammer or a rolled newspaper, but rather a book. It was thought, on the one hand, that in so doing one would rupture one side of the cyst, whereupon the goo within would be reabsorbed by the body; and that, on the other, the book's impact would be unlikely to cause the body any further damage.

Books can be used to apply the appropriate amount of pressure to things besides Bible bumps, for example, upon leaves intended for an herbarium, or damp dollar bills that one wants to dry out as smoothly as possible. Books are ultimately physical objects, and as such potential tools. They can be used to prop something up or keep it from wobbling, or to hold a window open just a crack. One can use books as coasters for wine glasses, or balance them on top of the head as part of physical therapy. And then, individual pages can be torn from them to be used for this or that—including, of course, certain unspeakable purposes.

However, all such uses throw a rather poor light on whoever practices, proposes, or tolerates them. The need must be fairly extreme, if one's ready to turn a book into a tool or first-aid kit. One generally suspects the perpetrator of being a boor, if not actually a fiend. And even in the case of the Bible bump, one always hopes (by the grace of God!) to find some alternative therapy, before having to reach for the Bible.

Our manner of dealing with books is quite rightly considered an indicator of mankind's relationship with culture as such. We can think of a text as a failure, or even as utterly wretched, and say so publicly, too. We can tear texts to pieces—but only metaphorically! Books, on the other hand, no matter what their content, must be treated with respect.

THE BURNED BOOK

I CAN KEEP this chapter brief. In his tragedy *Almansor*, written in 1821, Heinrich Heine crafted a handful of sentences on the subject to which almost nothing need be added.

In one scene, Almansor reports the following: "It came to our ears that the dreadful Ximenes, / Upon the market-square of great Granada—/ My very tongue does stiffen in revolt—/ Hurled the Koran upon a flaming pyre!" To which Hassan replies: "Such only proves that wherever books are burnt, / when all is said and done, men burn as well."

And so it happens, time and time again. It speaks against all hope for human progress that the Nazis began their own program of book-burnings—which have come to be seen as the *ne plus ultra* in the long history of this particular form of barbarism—less than a hundred years ago. In fact, this practice can be seen, symbolically, as prefiguring the Holocaust—and thus delivering the most gruesome imaginable confirmation of Heine's words.

ON THE TRADE

THE PRIMER

For several centuries, a person's life as a reader usually began with a primer. The primer—that is, a book by means of which one first learned to read—was our first encounter with printed texts. For plenty of people, the primer was, and remains, not merely their first but their *only* book; for many it remains unforgettable; for some, an awakening; for others, an agony.

Primers are brain-washings, both for good and ill. Insofar as they teach us to read, they create the requisite conditions for escaping immaturity, apathy, and prejudice. At the same time, primers cram the newly opened chambers of consciousness with texts, that all too often conflict directly with enlightenment. One has barely learned to read before being asked to fawn over some puppet or other or be made comfortable in sickly sweet fantasy-lands. The instrument that ought to lay the wide world open for our minds is turned awry—immediately serving to bar that world against us.

For decades, centuries, the primer has held and defended its dominion over the fledgling reader—its right, as it were, to those first and formative readings. It instituted and enforced the canon. Which is why there is such considerable and bitter strife over early readings. When political systems change, primers are immediately rewritten or replaced, often; they are fought over, reviled, ridiculed, and burnt.

In recent times, primers, at least in the Western world, have decidedly lost their prestige. By now, printed texts are ubiquitous. Even households that don't own a single book are plugged, via the internet, into the cosmos of the legible. And then there are other visual and acoustic media, which can in their own way tell stories even to those unable to read. They are establishing their *own* canon, and simultaneously dissolving the idea of one.

Thinking of all the many terrible primers there have been, we shouldn't grieve over their loss of power. Nevertheless, I feel sentimental, even apprehensive, when I see how in the midst of such a super- or overabundance of texts, the primer has lost its charisma. After all, it was once the first book of one's life. Leaving aside all of the silliness they've been filled with, they were *the* early key to a future of self-determination, one that promised every possibility. For anyone who learned to read from a primer, even those silly, naive, or pompous texts may remain in the memory as *vital* texts, as texts *par excellence*—as the first, and thus especially marvelous, experience of the fact that one can create, and derive, a world from words. One way or another, the primer was an event. If today texts creep rather *un*spectacularly into our lives, maybe something has indeed been lost.

THE DICTIONARY

When in the year 1838 the Brothers Grimm began their monstrous undertaking of a dictionary of the German language, did they have any suspicion that they wouldn't be capable of bringing it to fruition? The dictionary was originally envisioned as filling six or seven volumes, but in fact it finally ended in 1961 with the publication of the thirty-second. But as much as this project may have grown and sprawled over time, it was certainly always intended to be a finite one. When it reached the letter Z, it would be over. And indeed, so it happened.

All of this took place between 1838 and 1961—that is, during an era in which no lexicon or dictionary could be envisaged as anything other than a book, as a finite, well-defined mass of text. A book isn't a process, not multi-dimensional, not arbitrarily sprawling, not open on all sides, but rather something with a beginning, middle, and end. A book is a work, not a *working*; something made, not a *making*; a body, rather than a flux. It can be likened to a statue, a picture, a house, or a story—not a river, a dance, or a swarm.

Dictionaries are, in any case, books that aim to fix the world and hold it fast. Inasmuch as they clamp it between boards, they underscore the finitude of their subject. Dictionaries are an object of comfort, even when their volumes fill whole walls of shelves and you know you'll never be able to read them all. For dictionaries seem to say: "Don't worry. The world may be complex, but it's nevertheless containable. It may be huge, but look: it fits in a single room."

In short, dictionaries are a powerful balm for all those who find the world too variegated and confusing. Thousands upon thousands of dictionaries have stiffened the spines of men by displaying their own wide spines on living-room shelves, even if the edges of their pages remain layered with dust.

Of course, it must be acknowledged that the vision of such finite, firmly delineated knowledge no longer corresponds to contemporary consciousness. In plenty of disciplines, what had been established as fact is rendered obsolete within a year. The world is no longer suitable for dictionaries. And in consequence, the dictionary has become unworldly.

For many years, I personally relied on the Rowohlt *Dictionary of Film* (in six volumes). It stood within reach of my writing-desk. I would annotate specific articles with literary references, and—pedantically, perhaps—the death-dates of actors and directors. Moreover, I noted the dates on which I'd seen particular films, occasionally appending a brief rating. Bit by bit, the Rowohlt *Dictionary of Film* became a kind of guidebook to my life at the movies.

But years ago, I carried it down to the aforementioned basement, which would later be flooded. By then, you see, the internet had arrived—and the internet knew so much more about everything, including film. So—unhappily, with a heavy heart and guilty conscience—I parted with my handbook and, indeed, a piece of my history. Just as, long ago, so many farmers parted with their horses.

THE READING COPY

When a publishing house sets particular hopes on a new book, it has extra copies printed, usually with a simpler binding, and dispatches them gratis to critics and reviewers several months before the finished book is delivered. These books are referred to as "reading copies"—which is, truth be told, a fairly comical designation. As if the others, the "regular" copies, weren't intended to be read.

Be that as it may, reading copies are actually first editions, though they don't have a "genuine" first edition's aura. Is this because of the unsightly list of author appearances that most have emblazoned on their flyleaves? Or is it that they're de facto advertising tools, and as such tax-deductible? I'm not quite sure.

But I do know the strange allure that such reading copies exert, especially where I'm concerned. They were once, for a couple of weeks at least, books *before* the book. Strange as-ifs. Semi-public dress-rehearsals. Fetuses abroad in the world before the birth, preparing themselves for a life to come. Am I just saying that, or do I really sense in them the concentrated hopes of their creator? As much as I sense the grief that collects in them if those hopes are deceived or deserted, and the reading copy becomes its own grave.

THE FIRST EDITION

The essential function of a first edition is to accomplish a trick. This trick consists of getting the bibliophile to believe that the first edition is more valuable than any later edition of the book. And guess what: the trick works. It is substantially responsible for propping up a lion's share of the antiquarian book market.

But the question is, *how can* the trick work? Presumably in similar fashion to the trick with the book signed by its author: the first edition manages to suggest that it stands closer to the original text than later editions and printings. And the reader is happy enough to believe this, longing as he does for the original, for the primal aura, the unity of object and spirit.

All this is simply rubbish. Older first editions are often full of misprints, full of deviations from the manuscript. Plenty of first editions are simply constructs of their editors, who have, whether driven by ambition or anxiety, dramatically interfered with the text, or possibly patched it together or compiled it. And only years, decades, or centuries later may somebody make the effort to re-edit the text, bringing it closer, at last, to its source.

I own a couple of such "corrected" books, most of them of modern works, many even presenting transcriptions of manuscripts, including all deletions, insertions, or corrections. Poring over the printed page, the reader can get a sense of what the author must have once seen, staring down at his manuscript. Fascinating, admittedly.

However, for myself personally (and many others) first editions are slightly preferable for rather different reasons. On the one hand, of course, for reasons of collectors' pride. On the other hand, because when one looks down at the printed page, one sees just what the author would have seen, staring down at a leaf of his book fresh from the printer's. That moves me more.

THE PUBLIC READING COPY

I ENJOY watching my colleagues read aloud from their own books. If it were possible, I'd even love to look over their shoulders as they do it. I'm interested in the books, as well as the texts, from which they're reading.

In my experience, it's always the same copy they take with them to readings. Inside, there are notes, various pages marked with post-its; particular passages are underlined or struck out. Lines mark where to begin, where to skip ahead, and where to end. There are also corrections in the margins, marking typos overlooked by the proofreaders, or making significant improvements to a text which they've only come round to in the process of reading aloud. One can tell, by the partial discoloration of the edges of pages, precisely which passages are usually (or always) read. The dust jacket will have suffered considerably; the book spends plenty of time traveling in suitcases and pockets and hours on end in the grip of sweaty hands.

I sometimes think that the collecting of such copies marred by the hands of the author or continual reading constitutes the premier class of bibliophilia. But I can barely imagine that any author would give one of these copies up during their lifetime. In any case, *I* certainly wouldn't. For strictly sentimental reasons, naturally—but also because these reading copies reflect a piece of my history, my personal relationship to my own texts.

My early reading copies are conceived along the lines of poetry albums and decorated accordingly. In them I collected invitation cards to my readings, glued in photos, and at large gatherings of fellow writers, begged them all to write something inside. The texts themselves, on the other hand, I left unaltered, even those where a few little corrections would have improved them. I didn't correct a single typographical error, instead just putting up with them, even if they irritated me anew at every reading. Maybe I was simply happy to have finished a large text at all, so that laying a hand on it would have seemed a crime.

My later reading copies have a more prosaic air. I've added increasingly less personal or circumstantial material, instead noting and correcting whatever struck me amiss while reading. For example, I've removed various obstacles to live reading, such as the clashing of too many *ch* and *sch* sounds—because, given my native Rhenish accent, they led to errors. Above all, though, I've laid down a kind of musical score for my readings with the aid of dashes, lines, and arrows, just as I've frequently seen my fellow writers do. The goal is to make any jumps in the reading, when they're necessary, as inconspicuous as possible.

For a number of years, however, I've written hardly anything directly in a book. Instead, I've noted almost everything in a computer file: the various directions for reading, how much time the chosen passages will require, for what audience they're especially suited, and so on. I supplement these files each time I read, printing them out again. The page lies folded in the book, and then at the reading, discreetly beside it on the lectern.

Sadly, I'm forced to say: I do the above all out of caution. Once, I left a reading copy behind and didn't get it back; another time, one was simply stolen. That was bitter. Now, everything important is protected. Of course, the price is that my reading copies have become disposable, boring, without an aura.

Nevertheless, I wouldn't want to part with them.

BOOK ART

WHILE WAITING for one of my readings to start, I wander through the open auditorium. On display are works by the high school's upper classes. All of them examples of book-artworks. Of course I'm not sure if this is what they would call it. But you know what I mean: books painted, stuck together, dissected, arranged, tattered, and draped in various ways.

Here someone has built half a human being out of books, with an open book as a head of hair; clearly he was familiar with Arcimboldo's *Librarian*, or at least some art-teacher had introduced him to it. Beside it are books with nails through them, books in chains, and books partly embedded in concrete; I'm probably right in suspecting that I'm dealing with a critic of the suppression of free speech here. And then a couple of works that seem to belong to the category of the Japanese paper art of Origami.

I know, I shouldn't be ironic. First of all, students should be allowed to do almost anything, as long as they're learning. Furthermore, there's certainly a tradition of artistic work in the medium of the book. For example, a Dutch museum hosted a biennale of works on paper, and among other things displayed a thoroughly impressive piece: a kind of frozen waterfall of books, tumbling from the second story window of a house. Quite a few websites are devoted to "creative work with old books." And in English, as I've come to learn, "book art" seems to be an established notion, rather than an equivalent to the German word "Buchkunst."

But I have to be honest: I'm not especially fond of artworks made with books. Yes, there are certainly original and, above all, technically thrilling works in this genre; and I understand, too, that they represent an homage to the book, to language, to fantasy, and to the world of texts. Still, something in me protests. For to be able to become an artwork, a book's ability to function *as* a book is necessarily undone, even when the volume isn't completely destroyed. And although I've never found proof of it, I'm certain that, somewhere along the line, a one-of-a-kind book will be nailed or glued into a work of art.

Many years after the famous Soviet space mission during which the dog Laika perished in a tiny capsule, killed by heat and stress, one of the scientists involved expressed regret, saying: "We didn't learn enough through that mission to justify the death of a dog." Which is just how I feel about book art.

THE BOOK COLLECTION

THE PUBLIC LIBRARY

To PUT IT clearly and briefly: for a long time, libraries, when they didn't belong to monasteries or universities, were essentially subdivisions of princely treasure-chambers. The treasures of mind and spirit were housed alongside hoards of gold. Often enough the books were the property of people more interested in protecting their possessions than making use of them. It may be the case that plenty of other beautiful things arose during these ages: churches, castles, paintings, statues, music, and literature. One may well be glad their time is over.

For with the end of princely rule, many private treasuries of books were converted into public libraries. That was a tremendous service to the Enlightenment, among the most important steps towards the democratization of life in the West. Knowledge alone allows the public to have a say, and to appeal. Knowledge is power.

I knew none of this, nor would I have been very interested in it, at the age of nine when I received my borrower's card for the Mönchengladbach city library. Back then this institution was located, where it remains to this day, in an astonishingly peaceful section of the city center, only about two-hundred meters distant from the main shopping street, on the edge of a little park and surrounded by 19th-century townhouses. In those days, the building was brand new, not even three years old, as I've just learned from the library's website. It goes without saying that I didn't know any of this then—and I wouldn't have cared very much if I had.

Back in the winter of 1966–67, the building probably made no impression on me whatsoever. For a nine-year-old, it would have been no more than a roof over the heads of the books. And once you were inside, everything was completely self-explanatory. Just past the entrance there were little cabinets where I could store my schoolbag; a few steps beyond that was a bright room containing the children's and teens' section, through whose big windows one could look out on a peaceful green inner courtyard. The books stood ranked on shelves lit by sunshine from the courtyard, and you checked them out at a small counter beside the entrance. Beyond this, there was very little to interest me. Well, nothing but this: I would have liked to know how I could manage to check out a book from the shelves marked "12–14," despite my birth date being printed clearly on my library card, and a fairly strict librarian. I never attempted it, and instead bravely waited until I was 12. To make the time pass more quickly, I read almost all of the books on the "9–11" shelves.

The Mönchengladbach library, children's and teens' section, was the first library I ever encountered. At home we didn't possess a single book—until the day I received a whole load of them for my First Communion. None of our relatives or acquaintances owned a set of bookshelves or even a small bookcase. So what made me immediately recognize the library as the completely "right" place for me—indeed, as "my" place?

First, of course, the unbelievable heap of books that—assuming they weren't already on loan to someone—stood ready for me to take. Beyond that, I liked the library's atmosphere. Here was the exact opposite of the schoolyard: nobody ran, or ran riot. Nobody jostled me or jabbered at me, in order to make clear just how inferior I was. I treasured the library's tidiness and the sternness of its staff, despite the several years during which they forbid me access to the "12–14" shelf. I even enjoyed the protracted process of checking out books by hand, for which I had to stand in line. And finally, the lending periods, which divided my life so pleasantly into stretches of reading.

In the end, however, I developed a somewhat subversive streak among the stacks of the library. I knew that when I reached the age of sixteen, I'd finally gain access to the adult section—but I just couldn't wait. At thirteen or fourteen I persuaded my father to apply for a library card of his own. With this card in hand I immediately ventured into the adult section, which was many times larger than the children's, selecting my reading material by means of the brief descriptions on the backs of the books, and, finally, writing their titles in what I hoped was convincingly grown-up handwriting on a slip of paper. Then I checked them out—with my father's account, of course, and on his behalf. Each time I did this I shook like a swindler who simply can't believe that his trick is going to succeed again and again. But nobody ever investigated the matter, nobody even bothered to check the books against the slip of paper. And thus I have either the indifference or the wisdom of the staff of the Mönchengladbach public library to thank for the fact that, even before my sixteenth birthday, I was able to read through no mean amount of "grown up" literature.

Not long ago I heard that my first library had been awarded landmark status, as "an architectural testament to social change in West Germany after World War II. The openness, lucidity, and transparency of its structure" makes palpable "the value of an open, democratic society"—so go their stated grounds.

I subscribe to all these points with all my heart.

THE PRIVATE LIBRARY

On the Sunday after Easter in the year 1965, still a year and a half before the beginning of my career as a patron of the Mönchengladbach public library, I received at a single blow the first library of my own. It consisted in part of the usual communion gifts, but also of the belongings of a cousin more than ten years my senior. All told, there were about thirty books; among them a rather small dose of Karl May westerns, *The Leatherstocking Tales*, the legends of the ancient Greeks and Germans in editions for young readers, a very thick collection of Wilhelm Busch that quickly fell out of its fragile binding, and a children's visual dictionary, as well as a number of somewhat sedate children's books from the '50s, which my cousin had read through very gently.

After that Sunday, sad to say, my library grew rather slowly—or, to put it more accurately, not at all. In our family there was no tradition whatever of buying books, and when I, the first ambitious reader, made my appearance, my parents had a difficult time dealing with it. Membership in a book club was little help; but that's another story. Luckily, there was the public library. It made sense to me that checking out books was an economical alternative to purchasing them.

New additions to my library only arrived when I began my German classes in middle school; among them, of course, plenty of required reading, but also—finally!—books that neither the public library nor school had suggested to me. Somewhere along the line I'd overheard their titles, and now I bought them at the Boltze bookshop on Hindenburgstrasse, most of them with my skimpy allowance: Jack Kerouac's *On the Road*, William Burroughs' *Naked Lunch*, the previously-mentioned expensive volume on old sailing ships, and the satires of Ephraim Kishon.

In the spring of 1976, eleven years after that post-Easter Sunday of books, I moved into my first dorm room. I took along the books that I wasn't overly ashamed of, and I arranged them, as at home, on a rickety bookshelf from the 1960s that hung above my writing desk. It looked stuffy and pathetic up there, but it was really intended to spur me on. I had in fact moved into the room with the intention of building a library for myself. From the beginning, one wall was reserved for three inexpensive homemade bookcases, which in their shape anticipated Ikea's "Billy." And from my first day as a student I was buying books, as many as my means allowed, and sometimes more.

The intention of owning a "real" library has never left me. In the early years my efforts were directed above all toward bulk and great names; later I lapsed, swiftly and helplessly, into bibliophilia, or –mania. For years I made my purchases first and foremost in antiquarian shops and flea markets. Here there were plenty of bargains to be found and sometimes even remarkable finds.

Now books expanded around me in every direction. "A questionable mass," a doctor would call them. At first the shelves were supplemented with homemade constructions, then as more titles flowed into the room, other pieces of furniture had to make way. The wardrobe was moved out to the hallway—the bookshelves followed it out, and flanked it. When I got married and my wife and I moved into a shared apartment, I had to promise her beforehand that I'd restrict the books to my study; consequently, I was soon enough forced to arrange the books on my shelves in double rows, a solution that annoyed me terribly. I now scoured the flea markets for pieces of furniture—above all, little cupboards—that I could use, so to speak, as Trojan horses, to smuggle my books into the corridor and living room. Sometimes I succeeded, sometimes not.

We moved twice more, and the books moved with us. Once they got a lot of space in a sloping and half-lit appendix to an attic room, which wouldn't have been good for much else. But then they all had to be split into various sections and distributed across three different floors. When in 2000 I rented an apartment to use as an office and brought all of the books there with me, I took them from half a dozen different locations, including the hallway and a storage space underneath the roof. Then, for fourteen years, I had what I'd always dreamt of—a room filled with nothing but books! My perfect library! At first it seemed as if the shelves would never run out of space; but before long, of course they had to be expanded.

And everything could have remained just so. Yet whenever something in life seems certain, it's bound to change. Another move meant relinquishing the office apartment and brought me a new workroom, which, though it's nice and big, high and bright, is located under the roof, and so has almost no real wall-space to speak of. That is to say: a terrifying place for a book owner.

That would have been just the moment to make a clean—an exceedingly clean—break. Back when I bought my first books, computers were cupboard- or room-sized pieces of equipment from science-fiction films. But presently digital technology has made it possible to store ten thousand titles or more on a device smaller than a single book. For a moment I was tempted to hurl myself into the 21st century, to part ways with *all* my books, and begin building a new, digital library. Yet I let the moment pass—and then, with the help of a carpenter, I designed a kind of tower of books with a base about two square meters in area, which one can both walk through and climb, and with space for over eighty meters of shelving; or, to put it in other terms, around sixteen Billys.

Why am I telling you all of this? Only to prove that I've acquired a certain amount of expertise—albeit in a somewhat painful fashion—when it comes to reflecting upon the sense and nonsense of private libraries. Often enough over the years, usually while packing or unpacking boxes of books, I've asked myself what it really is that stands behind my desire to live surrounded by so many books?

And what has all this meditation and reflection yielded? The following answers.

FIRST: STOCKPILE

It may be that, fundamentally, book collecting is driven by the same impulses as other kinds of collecting: one wants to garner supplies for the sake of survival in lean times. Though today the fact seems to be largely forgotten (in this part of the world, at any rate) man was, for millennia, above all else a hunter and gatherer. And plenty of people remain so, even if what they're hunting and gathering are not rabbits and fruit but fads and collectibles.

So—is it that people today collect reading material as once they did food and firewood? The latter were necessary so that you wouldn't starve or freeze when the crops failed, and it was too cold or dangerous to go traipsing through the forest. Is the collecting of books then simply a species of intellectual stockpiling?

That was certainly the case at one point. And it even applied during the era in which I was first beginning to build up my library and when my contemporaries still hadn't been corrupted by visions of futuristic technologies for the storage of texts. The computer, as it existed then, was either unaffordable or the hobbyhorse of ambitious math-teachers. "Nerds" were still thought of as couch-potatoes, overachievers, or four-eyes; aside from their many paperbacks, the most advanced storage equipment they were likely to own was a tape-recorder.

And finally, no one shattered the mood of the sophisticated lover of literature with fantasies of e-books when, at the end of the day, as he waited for his red wine to reach room temperature, he browsed with pleasure among his bookshelves to select something appropriate for an evening's read.

But even then didn't the notion of stockpiling books have something touchingly antique about it? After all, the city-dweller of the 1980s lived in the midst of a dense network of retail bookstores and public libraries. For my part, I was at the university every day, no more than a doughty stone's throw away from its central library, and my walk to work led me right past the doors of the city's main library as well.

And since those days, books have become even easier to obtain. Today, online sellers deliver their wares as rapidly as the once-trusted physical bookstore, and moreover, direct to your doorstep. There's even a convenient digital marketplace for old, and very old, books; they've almost completely lost their status as lucky finds. Nowadays you hardly ever buy an old book out of the worry that you might never encounter another copy. Instead, in a matter of seconds, the internet presents you with the inventories of 3000 antiquarian booksellers from all over the world. What's more, the catalogs of most libraries are available online. And finally, there's the ongoing project—in principle highly enlightened, though at the same time somewhat creepy—of digitizing all the world's books in the public domain and placing them online.

In short: for several years now, anyone possessing

an internet connection, a modest bank account, and a mailbox, has been living in a virtual library whose holdings, while monstrously large, are simple to survey and easily dipped into. Compared to this cosmos of books, how modest appears the humble heap of paper on the bookshelves in a single apartment.

No, I'm afraid that I can't take the concept of stockpiling entirely seriously as a legitimate goal for the 21st-century personal library.

SECOND: STATUS SYMBOL

THE MIDDLE CLASSES usurped not merely the power of the princes, but a number of their customs, good as well as bad. There arose, as successors to the splendid salons of yesteryear, thousands of upper- and lower-middle-class living rooms, all heaped with "culture," just like their aristocratic role models. As shorthand for this hand-in-hand progression of economic achievement and propensity to culture, one might say: "property and education"; but sadly, the emphasis often fell on material goods—cultural property—rather than the Education of Man. When, for example, toward the end of the 19th century the classics entered the public domain, publishers flooded the market with luxury and collected editions which, most likely, rather than growing crooked and warped with excessive use, stood mute on their shelves, with their buckram spines turned toward the sitting rooms, stiff as the backs of those sitting rooms' residents.

Since at least 1968, there have been plenty of critics of the educated middle class's behavior vis-à-vis their cultural heritage. Yet bookcases and shelves have never quite shed their nimbus. Even today one never asks the owner of numerous books if he's read and understood them all; as a rule, one takes their mere presence as evidence of his education and appreciation of literature.

Just as owning a dog doesn't imply that one has a universal love of animals (often enough the exact opposite is the case). Yet hardly anyone believes that somebody with a strong aversion to all things intellectual would purchase and live among thousands of books.

This buckling before the mere existence of bookshelves might seem naïve, but nonetheless it signals something positive. Clearly the book can be considered a kind of fundamentally ethical object, even if there are, as is well known, plenty of books whose reading doesn't necessarily make one a better human being.

So: was I myself (and am I still) one of those people whose ideal image of themselves is set against a backdrop of bookshelves? Just as in earlier eras the industrialist would have his portrait painted before his factory, or the captain before his ship? This raises fears of vanity—albeit a widespread and socially-acceptable sort of vanity. For even in the age of digitalization the bookshelf remains a popular and beloved icon. Every day, thousands of scientists, clergymen, artists, and politicians are posed by photographers and cameramen before bookshelves, patently in hopes that their filmed ten-second-statements will thereby somehow gain in gravity. A world growing faster day by day stands in desperate need of such unambiguous signs. To this day, the bookshelf seems to serve that particular end. And need.

And above all, of course, for its owner.

THIRD: COLLECTION

One can collect books the way one collects stamps or beer-coasters—that is, purely as objects. In which case their role as intermediary between text and reader plays no part. Stamps are often only the objects of a collection after they've become completely useless—for instance, because they've outlived their countries. And collectors of beer coasters are careful not to set damp glasses on them.

Though intact books never quite become entirely useless, one can nevertheless consider them strictly as objects, never even read them, and still treasure and collect them. For example, one might amass books from a certain era, or literary tendency, or publisher, set them one beside the other on a shelf, and thus give physical expression to an intellectual abstraction, like the fairy tale, or Dada.

I myself own almost all of the books that Karl Kraus tears to pieces in his polemic *Literature Demolished* from 1896. I've barely read any of them; Kraus himself has emphatically communicated to me that it wouldn't be worth my time. Nevertheless, I take pleasure in having his whole satirical panopticon arrayed before me. As I've already mentioned, for some time I've collected signed books, because I believe that they give off a kind of aura. And to my own astonishment, I've returned—after a lapse—with fresh zeal to my task of completing my collection of books by Peter Altenberg.

All things considered, however, these collections are only small, perhaps somewhat quirky preserves within my current library. Were my stock of books composed solely of such dead or at least deeply slumbering paper I'd feel profoundly uncomfortable with myself. At the same time, I get along well with all collectors—even those who aren't readers. Collecting means giving order to something, inasmuch as one brings together those things that one feels belong together. And as long as one doesn't commit theft or murder in the process, that isn't the worst way to employ one's mind or money.

FOURTH: ARCHIVE

I'VE PLACED this particular result of my ruminations at the tail end of the list because, since the most recent (and hopefully final) experience of moving my library, I feel that, for me at least, it carries the most weight. When once again it was time to decide which books would come along and which would remain behind, it became clear to me that above all I want to be surrounded by books to which I'm bound by something substantial—no, not simply their texts, but something even more important: their readings.

In fact, after years of purchases and collecting, my library has become a repository of books that I've already read. I know, of course, that this is nothing particularly original; plenty of private libraries have evolved along similar lines, whether in whole or part, and more or less purposefully. Yet if one ponders this seemingly self-evident idea for a little bit longer, one finds it confusing.

Because it could be entirely otherwise. Years ago I heard an anecdote about a young professor of literature at an American university, who, whenever you asked him about his library, would hold up a single paperback and say, "*This* is my library"; and whenever he finished that book, would give or throw it away. I think the story was set in Berkeley in 1968. When I first heard it, it gave me the creeps, but, along with his strained anti-bourgeois attitude, the young professor also demonstrated a certain common sense. For how rarely do we actually read a book a second time! Sure, every ambitious work really demands a deeper reading; yet often enough we prefer to devote what remains of our inexorably accelerating lives to something fresh, rather than immersing ourselves in the familiar. We may repeatedly consult dictionaries and guidebooks, but the lion's share of beautiful literature falls, after we've finished reading it, into a deep slumber.

Yet despite this, books we've read generally don't wind up with a friend, or in the dumpster. Rather, they're set on a bookshelf where together with others, bit by bit, they grow over the walls like paper ivy. And it's pleasant to see them there, too. I believe that the read book maintains its value because it's a visible, tangible document of one's life as a reader. And in that sense, it doesn't matter in the least whether or not it's read a second time.

A read book is a piece of a reader's history. A book—or maybe even a particular passage from one of its most important chapters, one of those places where the reader would have loved to remain, where one felt most at home. Every text is a world of language, and at the same time, for the reader, a diary of his or her journey through that world. Thus the book is preserved like a travel journal, able to relive that journey from time to time in memory. And as with travel journals, often its mere presence suffices to keep those memories alive.

The personal library is thus the archive of a reading life. Or perhaps a mausoleum in which, though sealed away, one lives like nowhere else.

THE BOOKSTORE

Bookstores may resemble libraries, but they're nothing of the kind. They're more like way-stations, short-term harbors for books on their journeys to the reader or toward still other shelves. Here, too, the books are perfectly ordered—but with a kind of train station or airport order, which above all else (or, rather, only) serves the goal of expediting transfer. In the bookstore, no book is allowed to grow old; instead, everything drives on toward change. Depending on the season, holiday, media hype, or bestseller-list, the piles of books can be swapped with lightning speed, shelves emptied and newly filled again.

Bookstores are forums, taverns, and marketplaces for those interested in texts. Here one can keep oneself informed, ferret out the newest sensations, the most ancient wisdom, and the usual gossip. Moreover, one can take the wares in one's hand and engage in various kinds of deliberation: canvass the blurbs on the jacket, appreciate the illustrations, read through a specimen page. For those with good memories, formulas and poems even lend themselves to theft—and without any possibility of cops interfering.

Incidentally, at one point it was common enough to find bookstores that didn't merely *look* like libraries. They actually *were* libraries—highly personal collections, established and curated by their owners. Stepping into such shops meant penetrating the distinctly individual reading world of the bookseller, possibly with a less than entirely pleasant sensation, since one was always afraid of disturbing the Master or Mistress of the place while he or she was reading or organizing the stock. Buying a book here felt like tearing a hole in a painstakingly composed cosmos in which the rules of the market, the favorites of the season, played a restricted role, or possibly none whatsoever. If one could bring oneself to commit such an enormity, one generally received, whether one wanted it or not, the owner's commentary on the chosen book, free of charge.

But such bookstores have become rare, and may be facing extinction. Sad. They were already few and far between when I first began buying books, and today there are big cities where none of their species can be found at all. In the '70s and '80s, there were still newly opened bookstores that catered to particular interests: bookstores for women, for children, for gays and lesbians, for those keen on the occult or the adherents of various religions. Even today you find people behind the counters with purposes that extend beyond the merely economic—merchants with principles. Yet these types, too, have long been in the minority.

More than twenty years ago, as a young man, I was lucky enough to meet one of those old-school booksellers. I was reading from my first book of stories in a small Westphalian city. For the event, the bookseller, only a few years younger than I was, had me sign thirty copies of my book. When I asked if this wasn't a bit optimistic, he said with total seriousness and without a trace of irony: "The people around here buy what I recommend."

I just looked the place up on the internet: that bookshop is still there, and while the bookseller's beard has grown longer, it's as red as ever. I wish him all the best!

THE ANTIQUARIAN

ANTIQUARIAN SHOPS are bookstores from which time has withdrawn. Here there is no seasonal trade, no ephemeral goods on bestseller tables. The books in an antiquarian shop have all (or almost all) been bought before, some of them many times over. On the front and rear flyleaves are prices in various currencies, some of them, probably, no longer in circulation. Nobody advertises these books anymore. And most of them have shed their dust jackets along with all pretense of fashion or marketability. Like the bookstore, the antiquarian shop is also a place of transit, but here the waiting no longer makes anyone nervous—indeed, it seems as if waiting has become a better, or at least a more dignified, kind of existence.

Like the new bookstore, the antiquarian shop is sought out both by those who know what they're looking for, and those who are content to be counseled or surprised. One type of shopper, however, is found *only* at the antiquarian shop: the manic treasure-hunter. He carries around with him a long hit-list of fantasy finds, and wanders the world of paper in his quest to make them real. The notion that on these very shelves some long-sought book is waiting for him (and for him alone) intoxicates and electrifies him. Yet such a coup would be surpassed by the discovery of a book which this bibliophile soldier-of-fortune has never even heard of, and which would immediately take pride of place as the centerpiece of his collection.

One can like, perhaps even love, bookstores—but antiquarian shops, on the contrary, either repel you or you grow completely addicted. I undertook my most thrilling expeditions in the early '80s in Vienna, probably the last city in central Europe where there are still antiquarian shops that resemble catacombs, resting-places for undead books that slumber for decades till a reader ransoms them.

There in Vienna I met one antiquarian who has ever since epitomized the breed for me. When he saw which books I was interested in, he told me, rapturously, and with tremendous vividness, how as a young man in the 1930s he had gone to Karl Kraus's readings. It was as if I'd been touched by a draft from the casket of literary history in that dusty store. And just like that, this man seduced me into purchasing a pair of expensive first editions. When I hesitated, he even claimed that he couldn't bear to part with the books, they carried too many memories. In the course of a single afternoon, a single encounter, I had spent practically all the money I'd brought on my trip.

Incidentally, this man lived in a tiny appendix to his shop. I could see into it through a half-open door. It was filthy in there, heaps of books towered above a kind of folding cot. Books lay on a little table beside a coffee pot and a cup. The shop itself was likewise so bursting with books that I could barely navigate it. Piles of books lay in front of every shelf, and I had to shift them aside in order to browse. Where that wasn't possible, I needed to twist myself down in order to decipher the titles on their spines. On the sagging boards the books were wedged so tightly that you couldn't pull one out without fearing that the others would come tumbling out on you as well.

Before that, I'd always thought that book dust wouldn't smell at all; but here I learned: it certainly does. It smells powerfully, and its odor can terrify.

THE BOOKMOBILE

In both of the little suburbs where I grew up, fresh bread was delivered each morning; moreover, a baker regularly made the rounds with pies and Danish pastries, along with a dealer in eggs and poultry, and another for beer and lemonade. During the summer the so-called "little ice man" had his place on the corner and was always eagerly awaited. And I'd almost forgotten: there was a junkman, who also hauled away old paper. Generally, they all announced themselves with a bell, or by honking a horn. All that was missing was a bookmobile to supply us with reading material.

However, I have no regrets on that front. It might, in some sense or other, have been a boon to have been provided with a mobile library. But then I would have lost my primary excuse for leaving those two little suburbs and heading into the city.

Today the sight of a bookmobile leaves me feeling melancholy. You can still see the good intentions behind it: popular enlightenment. The first examples in 19th-century Europe—at that time drawn by horses—furnished reading material, and thereby the building-blocks of self-consciousness, to the homes of people who lacked the time and energy to seek out public libraries. Their heyday came in the mid-20th century, when the provision of intellectual nourishment attained the position of a mandatory government benefit.

Elsewhere in the world, mobile libraries still remain a highly sensible thing. I've read about mules and camels that, in South America and Africa respectively, transport books to their readers. Here in Europe, meanwhile, bookmobiles are touchingly outmoded, frightfully concrete equivalents to, and reminders of, the internet. They demonstrate how much energy and effort is required to transport, say, three thousand books from one place to another. Meanwhile, an untold mass of digitized texts can arrive in the space of seconds anywhere at all, as long as there's an appropriate device to receive them. A man with three books in his hand, waiting at the stop for the bookmobile in order to exchange them for three others is a living fossil, and still a sight that can move you to tears.

THE BOOKSHELF

For genuine, honest-to-goodness bibliomaniacs, it's all the same to them where their books are housed. It *has* to be all the same to them, since they no longer have time to fuss over the upkeep of their possessions. They're addicts, and as with all addictions, so with books—one is constantly forced to increase the dosage. So sometimes the books spill from their shelves, pile up on the floor, mount unstoppably against empty walls, becoming in the end their own sort of furniture, and ultimately, perhaps, the only furniture their owner possesses.

In milder cases of bibliophilia, on the other hand, the billeting of books still plays a more important role. Here a good deal of money (given the simplicity of its purpose) is lavished on the design of appropriate furniture. Rococo and classical bookshelves often have something precious, even shrine-like about them, while those from bourgeois eras occasionally resemble fortresses to protect intellectual valuables.

The modern era, however, has largely put an end to boxing-in books and settled instead on open shelving; nowadays the Billy and its derivatives provide a kind of minimal standard for storing books. Meanwhile, many people consider it almost poor taste to set books on furniture with any aesthetic aspiration, rather than nobly and discreetly ceding the foreground to its contents.

At the same time, anyone who wants to can still furnish himself and his books in the style that was common in an earlier era. One can, for instance, purchase replicas of the Elastic Bookcase, patented by the Globe-Wernicke company in 1897: extendible bookcases, with glass doors if desired, built of individual components, and easily disassembled. I imagine how, once upon a time, white colonial officials would have transported them, along with furniture and foodstuffs, from one foreign posting to another. These days, however, such cabinets are probably almost never purchased by people on the move. They're more likely to find favor among those who believe that a noble and spiritual lifestyle is impossible to achieve with 20th- or 21st-century furniture.

Yet even in progressive or alternative circles, bookshelves—especially those in the living room—are still a favorite furnishing, with an identity of its own. You can't go wrong with a simple set of bookshelves. They stand firm and assert themselves, without getting lost in the whirlpool of hectic individualization and diversification. Next door in the kitchen, as far as cooking and eating go, it's every man for himself—from veganism to microwave dinners, Thai food to haute cuisine. One prefers endurance- or high-performance training or yoga, or nothing at all—and everyone, naturally, has his or her own style. One smokes or drinks or vaporizes, or none of these. Anyone who buys a car or a laptop immediately earns a rueful shake of the head from his acquaintances: always the wrong make or model. And anyone who furnishes his new flat only provides a chamber of horror for his guests.

For that, the simplest possible bookshelf is always the advisable lifesaver. It's perhaps the only type of furnishing that doesn't fall prey to great aesthetic, ethical, or moral qualms, or questions. It radiates a peculiar kind of warmth, perhaps even that of its owner, and exudes a sense of simultaneous privacy and openness, of character and function, that constitutes every living human being. What other piece of furniture can do all that? I can't think of a single one.

CONCLUSION

THAT'S IT. Of course I haven't exhaustively compiled all the qualities and "behavioral patterns" of books, but I won't let that bother me. On the contrary, I'd be delighted if you, my reader, would add your own supplements, perhaps in pencil on a blank page. Just this once, I won't hold it against you.

By the time this book is published, I'll be looking my 60th birthday in the eye. Which means that I'll probably pass the rest of my life in a mélange of paper and digital texts. Still, I'm surrounded by people who categorically refuse to read long and, especially, literary texts on monitors or screens. In my age group, they remain the majority. But I have an acquaintance of my own age who credibly assures me that for weeks now he's been reading Proust's *In Search of Lost Time* on his smartphone. And that it was precisely this "format" that allowed him to read it for the first time; these days he reads not only in bed or on the train, but every minute of his day during which he'd otherwise merely be waiting.

When I told this to my sons, with an undertone of surprise, they didn't understand me. The people who've grown up with computers, the "digital natives," are totally accomplished when it comes to writing and reading digital messages. For many of them the book is already an antiquated, almost exotic, medium, even when they have a close relationship to various kinds of texts, including literature.

If I take myself as an example, all the turmoil of the contemporary situation is revealed. On the one hand, I don't own a single e-book reader, even though I fret terribly over bringing insufficient or unsuitable reading material with me on vacation. On the other hand, ever since I began working as a writer, my workplace has included a PC. For every one or two hours per day that I spend reading books, there are six, or eight, or ten, in which I'm writing or correcting my texts, researching on the internet, reading and composing emails, or drifting around in forums devoted to various causes. Clearly I'm a typical "digital immigrant"—which is to say, I first experienced the digital world as an adult, but since then have found my life decisively shaped by it. Despite this, I cling firmly to certain reading and textual habits of my youth, considering most of them as "normal," although they nowadays play only a subordinate role.

So one of the reasons I've written this book is simply to pause for once, to look more closely at what I've always assumed was the obvious medium for texts: the book. Some of my observations have been quite personal. I can't help that, and I wouldn't want to. Books today seem to be enjoying a peaceful stasis, seem to stand so self-effacingly on their shelves. But in truth, they're the bearers of messages that only spring to life when the books are sought out, purchased, and—of course—read. The material worth of a book might be calculated in the publisher's office or the auction-house, but their actual value is dictated by the relationships they sustain with their readers. Which is why I've occasionally been my own subject here. I certainly hope—no, I'm sure—that my readers will write themselves into the text; that is, that they'll summon up and commit to writing their own experiences with books.

After the first reading, my publisher called my text "melancholy." And I think that's probably true of my mood as well. As I said earlier, I wouldn't survive an absolute End of the Book, were such an event to occur. But I've already experienced the gradual decline of a key medium, and thus the waning of a world which, during the first half of my life, I assumed was irreplaceable. That may sound melancholy, akin to the knowledge that one is growing older, and the finiteness of life becomes perceptible.

Nevertheless, I hope that I haven't written a *pessimistic* book. I know well enough that plenty of the qualities of printed books have no counterpart in the e-book. For example, what will happen to the book signing, to the borrowed book, to the first edition, to the bookstore, when texts float from place to place as data? Will people still give novels as gifts, and if so, how? But just because I don't know what kind of text-culture the e-book will supply to replace the book culture we have shouldn't lead me to assume that the answer is *none*. In one of my history classes—it must have been back around 1968—the teacher read us a text on the decline of culture in the younger generation. It might have been written by one of our contemporaries, but it came instead from ancient Egypt. The older generation has always enjoyed styling itself as the last, the very last, guardians of culture. And then the next generation does it again, and the generation after that, and so on.

Which doesn't imply that one should simply look on in silence. If the e-book strongly favors a particular type of literature while making matters more difficult for another, one has to step in. If digital culture transforms the text into the kind of commodity you pay for according to the exact amount you consume, like water, gas, and electricity, then one has to protest. And if writers and booksellers are being deprived of a livelihood in the process, all the more reason to do so.

I hope this won't happen. The overwhelming majority of book lovers are also lovers of texts. And even if we are actually able to give up printed books as we gave up horses, it wouldn't mean that we could get along without meaningful texts. *That* I simply cannot imagine.

THE WRONG BOOK

OFTEN ENOUGH, the wrong book simply can't help it. Perhaps it was merely in the wrong place at the wrong time. Or we followed a bad recommendation, or didn't understand the recommendation correctly, or wrote it down *in*correctly. In any case: the wrong book is an irritation, one that you'd gladly get rid of. Yet as a physical object, it asserts its presence; it isn't so simple to remove this mistake from your world.

Of course, you can try. For example, by putting the wrong book in a holding pattern on the nightstand. Perhaps the eye's familiarity with the wrong book will eventually convert it to the right one. Or you can inter it in a bookcase, so that time will accomplish the same feat unaided. On the other hand, you can take action and give the book away, or lend it to someone, ridding yourself of the memory of the error.

Wrong books are especially bad when they supplant right books. Unfortunately this happens frequently on trips or during vacations, especially on so-called (or actual) deserted islands. There, the right book is, for a while at least, inaccessible, and immediately the wrong book becomes (for hours, days, or weeks) a painful reminder that you've (yet again) played fast and loose with your limited time for reading and living. And then the wrong book may well become the focus of all the